QATAR'S SHADOW WAR

The Islamist Emirate and its

Information Operations in the United States

DAVID REABOI

CENTER FOR SECURITY POLICY PRESS

Copyright © 2021 by David Reaboi

All rights reserved. No part of this publication may be re-produced or transmitted in any form or by any means electronic or mechanical, including photocopy, recording, or any in-formation storage and retrieval system now known or to be in-vented, without permission in writing from the publisher, except by a reviewer who wishes to quote brief passages in connection with a review written for inclusion in a magazine, newspaper, website, or broadcast.

Cover illustration: **Leigh Brown**
Leighandbrown@protonmail.com
@leighandbrown

Design: David Reaboi

ISBN: 9798712666737

Published in the United States by Center for Security Policy Press

Manufactured in the United States of America

CONTENTS

Introduction

The New Middle East

"Universal Values" from Bush to Obama

Designated Heroes and Villains

Donald Trump in the New Middle East

Qatar, the Islamist Emirate

The Wahhabbis and the Ikhwanis

The English and the Americans

The Anatomy of Information Operations

Lessons from the Hoax

The Media's Collapse and Rebirth as 'Echo Chamber'

American Media in the Service of Qatar

Qatar's Own Media Assets

Experts and Talking Heads

Oppo Shops and Lobbyists

The Operation's Political Goals

Epilogue

Policy Suggestions

Notes

INTRODUCTION

This short book is about Qatar, a country from where Islamists of the Muslim Brotherhood are able to use tremendous oil and natural gas wealth to promote the Brotherhood's ideology around the world.

Using this political warfare infrastructure, Qatar also advances its own national interests against its chief regional rival, Saudi Arabia, as it bucks to replace one of America's most important strategic alliances. Due to their policy biases and the friendly intellectual environment created and nurtured by petrodollars inside the Beltway, American elites and policymakers have been soft targets for Qatari influence and information operations.

In the 1960s, Gamel Abdel Nasser banned and cracked down on the Brotherhood in Egypt, forcing thousands of the group's agitators, clerics and community organizers to retreat elsewhere into the Middle East, Europe, and North America. Since then, Qatar has been a tiny oasis for Hamas' ideological mothership, the Muslim Brotherhood, and many of the world's most virulent Islamists.

In time, Brotherhood Islamism would soon emerge as Qatar's defacto state ideology, as the ruling al-Thani family welcomed the Islamists with lavish funding, the highest state honors, and the establishment of new Islamist institutions that would indoctrinate thousands of extremist clerics. It funds and provides sanctuary to the bloodthirsty designated terror group Hamas,[1] and is relentlessly hostile to American interests.[2]

In addition to supporting terrorism against our allies in Israel, Qatar has used its powerful media infrastructure to topple our Arab allies in the Middle East by fomenting revolution within our their borders.[3] With the turn of Gulf states like Saudi Arabia and against Islamism, Qatar is today the last major state patron for Brotherhood activists and groups, especially in the West.[4]

Qatar has been exceptionally successful at buying and obtaining influence to advance its interests in Washington. The extent of its influence and information operations is one of the least-covered and least-scrutinized stories of the last few years but, thankfully, that's changing. Because of its promotion of the Muslim Brotherhood and its alliance with Iran, more and more American are coming to understand that Qatar is a malign force—not just in the Middle East but in this country, as well.

Of course, spending a lot of money is the easiest way to change or tweak a public policy narrative. Having great wealth allows you to gain friends instantly, in the hope that your generosity will enrich these new friends as well. Nations spend a lot of money in the United States to advance their interests; rich nations, of course, can afford to spend more lavishly.

But not every foreign dollar spent on making a nation's voice heard inside the Beltway is equal: there are a number of pro-American allies that advance a policy agenda that aligns with U.S. national security and economic interests. There are, on the other hand, countries that pay enormous sums of money to influence American policy against our interests. The policies these nations pursue can do real harm to our country's welfare, both here and abroad. Because of its position with respect to terrorism, its alliance with Iran and Sunni Islamism, the millions of dollars Qatar has spent trying to influence perceptions and policies here in Washington falls squarely into this latter, more dangerous category.[5]

Qatar's vast wealth can alter policy by carefully manipulating narratives and perceptions using weaponized information in the United States. The sums of money are so large—and the effort to evade the Foreign Agent Registration Act (FARA) and other disclosure laws are so comprehensive—that we don't have anywhere near a complete picture of the scope of Qatar's influence game. What we do know is worrying enough:

Qatar's money has been able to buy lobbyists who have "encouraged" a number of influential people to soften their line on Qatar's support for terrorism and Islamism or take up rhetorical arms against its chief regional rivals, especially Saudi Arabia and the United Arab Emirates.

It's been able to buy media outlets that create the battlespace or the environment that leads, as we have seen, in very short order, to dramatic policy shifts designed to benefit Qatar.

And it's been able to cement pro-Qatar narratives in the minds of the professional Beltway foreign policy elite through massive grants to think tanks, universities and, perhaps most troublingly, shrewd use of the CENTCOM base at al-Udeid as a platform from where Qatar could ingratiate itself to a generation of U.S. military commanders and policymakers.

THE NEW MIDDLE EAST

In a recent dramatic defeat—and a startling win for the Trump administration—the Brotherhood was powerless to stop the diplomatic thaw between Israel and its neighbors in the region. In August 2020, the Emirates and Israel embarked on a path toward normalized relations, signing the Abraham Accords at the White House in Washington. In short order, more Muslim states agreed to normalize relations with the Jewish State; Bahrain, Sudan, Morocco and other states soon followed.

Today, the Israeli wine and other products for sale in Dubai and Abu Dhabi supermarkets serve as a definitive rebuke to the strength of the anti-Israel Boycott, Divestment and Sanctions (BDS) campaign. If even the most prominent Muslim countries in the world do not boycott goods produced in the Jewish State—and, instead, proudly celebrate the emergence of real peace and cooperation, how could European nations justify anti-Israel boycotts? It must be doubly infuriating for the Muslim Brotherhood, as the primary organizational driver of BDS in the United States is affiliated with that has been spearheaded and funded by American Muslims for Palestine, a group that exists largely on the ruins of the now-outlawed, Hamas-funding Holy Land Foundation.[6]

The Abraham Accords, as well as the larger trend toward peace, non-enmity, and genuine coexistence between Muslims and Jews in the Middle East, is a massive blow to Islamists. The Brotherhood's project, as part of a transnational Islamist revival movement in the early 20th Century, has largely focused on what Qatar-based Brotherhood leader Yusuf al-Qaradawi calls, the "Islamic Awakening." In different and complimentary ways these last several decades, both Qaradawi and Osama bin Laden's al Qaeda sought to heighten the religious conflict between the Muslim and non-Muslim worlds by emphasizing an exclusive Islamic religious identity that necessarily puts it in conflict with non-Muslims. Using a mix of resentment, grievance, terror attacks, as well as a strong focus on building fundamentalist networks of diaspora Muslims in the West, this "Awakening" would, the Islamists hoped, radicalize and activate the Islamic ummah worldwide to work toward an eschatological goal. The attacks of 9/11—as well as the anticipated robust response from the United States—were intended to be the inciting event for this new, radical consciousness of the world's Muslims.

The high point of the "Islamic Awakening" was the Arab Spring in 2011. The uprisings throughout the Middle East and North Africa were instigated by Qatar's state sponsored al Jazeera network, and served to advance the interests of well-prepared and organized Muslim Brotherhood factions in the region. Al Jazeera presented and hyped the protests throughout the Arabic-speaking world, using photogenic and sympathetic young liberal protesters to ignite protests in Egypt, Libya, Tunisia and elsewhere. In each case, an effectively anti-Islamist government was toppled by Western-supported protesters and replaced with Islamists. This maneuver was attempted in Syria, as well, but it didn't work out the way the Islamists had hoped. There, massive anti-regime protests caused a civil war; civil society in Syria would collapse and, subsequently, draw Iran, the United States, Turkey, al Qaeda, ISIS, and Russia into a messy maelstrom that still vexes the world's foreign policy elite—who are, unsurprisingly, united in thinking the region would be better off with Islamists governing the country.

In Saudi Arabia and the United Arab Emirates, the wave of destruction in the wake of the Arab Spring was clear. While the oil-rich Gulf monarchies had long been the targets of Islamists, the Arab Spring was a frightening reminder of what the Muslim Brotherhood was capable of. They began to push back on the Brotherhood, which meant pushing back on the group's most important and wealthy patron, Qatar.

The Arab anti-Islamist counter-offensive was not limited to the Gulf. Within several years, the Brotherhood was sent reeling. The Islamist government of Mohamed Morsi in Egypt disappeared in 2013, just as if it had never existed. The Islamic State (ISIS) in the Levant and North Africa are no longer actors on the global stage, commanding headlines for terror attacks and brutality. Sudan's longtime Islamist dictator rots in prison, awaiting trial. Saudi Arabia and the Emirates banned the Brotherhood's operations on their soil and have halted funding to Islamist groups. The UAE has even designated American fronts for the Islamist group as terrorist organizations. Today, the Brotherhood is stronger in the West than in any predominantly Muslim country in the East, save one: Qatar.

"UNIVERSAL VALUES" FROM BUSH TO OBAMA

For many in the United States—especially those within the Beltway foreign policy elite—this was not how things were supposed to work out.

Following 9/11, a consensus had formed in order to explain the nature and dynamics of the conflict between the West and Islamist terror groups. In this reading, the Islamists' goals, motives, and doctrines were immaterial; the spasms of violent Islamic terrorism unleashed on the West are merely the product of authoritarian societies in the Middle East and their citizens' lack of freedom to pursue their religiously inspired political aspirations peacefully at the ballot box.[7] This analysis took for granted that fairly-elected Islamists better represented the will of the populations of Muslim-majority countries than either the pro-

American autocrats or monarchies with which the United States had long-standing alliances.

"Democracy" and "freedom" became buzzwords, aspirations—and soon, the earnest policy goals within both elite foreign policy circles and national security bureaucracies. Logic seemed to dictate, then, that support for "democracy" and "freedom" in the Middle East would, necessarily, translate into de facto support for various local tribunes of political Islam, especially the Muslim Brotherhood. Since Islamists were the immediate beneficiaries of a democratization policy, the elites were disposed to consider nearly all Islamist movements "moderate." A bipartisan consensus on this issue turned this theory into a touchstone concept of both Bush and Obama administration policy. In this way, promoting Islamist groups had, over time, come to define the American national interest.

Since the Eisenhower administration, the Brotherhood has long been a favored interlocutor for western diplomats, the intelligence community, think tanks and others, on both sides of America's partisan divide. It's worth exploring how two different ideologies interact with Islamists in US foreign policy.

While the Bush administration was caricatured as being belligerent, war-hungry and anti-Muslim by both the Left and Islamists, the truth is far different. What united many of the Bush-supporting neoconservatives of that era wasn't a willingness to use force against America's enemies; that position has always been uncontroversial in the United States. This country has a long Jacksonian tradition that traditionally waxes and wanes, but always reasserts itself. After 9/11, nearly all conservatives (together with the vast majority of Americans) sought a robust reprisal for al Qaeda forces and the states which harbored and supported them. But it was the neoconservatives' assumptions about human nature that pulled them in different—and eventually unsustainable—policy directions.

"We go forward with complete confidence in the eventual triumph of freedom," President Bush proclaimed in his second inaugural address in January 2005. "Not because history runs on the wheels of inevitability.... We have confidence because freedom is the permanent hope of mankind; the hunger [in the] dark places; the longing of the soul."

The words are stirring, and perhaps the sentiment is beautiful. But is it true? Even within the confines of the United States, looking at our own fellow citizens, our definitions of freedom couldn't be more different. And, in the near two decades since that speech was given, the hollowness of Bush's statement has shown to be less naïve than delusional. When transferred onto humanity at large—a massive stage that includes so many different cultures and, hence, different ways of understanding "freedom"—and then used as the theoretical engine that drives policy for the most powerful nation on earth—the delusion is compounded into tragedy, and then malpractice.

It turned out that neoconservatives were and are ideologues who believe in "universal values" which transcend culture, religion and everything else. The "universal values" dogma wasn't merely the engine that propelled the Bush administration into prosecuting wars in Afghanistan and Iraq in a disastrous and counterproductive way—it was also the ideological force behind so much neoconservative economic and immigration policy, as well. After all, if human beings had, essentially, the same base desires—for "freedom," as any number of former Weekly Standard writers would define it—all people are basically interchangeable.

All this would come as a great relief to philosophers and theologians from the beginning of time who wrestled seriously with these questions.

Of course, this is a profoundly shallow way of seeing the world, and it has had terrible consequences for everyone involved. The "Freedom

Agenda" articulated in Bush's Second Inaugural set the stage for policies that must inevitably benefit Islamists, both in the Middle East and domestically.

After the terror attacks in September 2001, the Bush administration found, correctly, that it needed to define the enemy it was now fighting. Rather than approach the jihadist enemy based on its own published doctrine, it believed that such a definition of the threat would compromise its ability to prosecute the war and alienate potential Muslim allies. On one hand, it refused to hold accountable the Arab states involved in generating pro-Islamist propaganda and justification for attacks; on the other, it undermined the stability of those states by urging them to adopt various democratic gestures without the essential bulwark of a civil society.

Because all people have "universal values," the anti-American, anti-Western attitudes of the so-called Arab Street had to be the product of political dysfunction alone. If "freedom" was what was in every man's heart, the lack of political expression for that "freedom" in the Middle East, they believed, created the conditions for intra-civilizational conflict, bloodshed and war.

And so, in the most celebrated case—a spectacularly self-contained strategic and tactical failure, if there ever was one—the Bush administration, at the urging of then-Secretary of State Condoleezza Rice, pushed the Israelis to table their objections to the designated terrorist group Hamas' presence on the ballot in the 2006 Gaza elections. The Palestinians, free of Israeli occupation after Prime Minister Sharon's contentious withdrawal from the territory a year earlier, were now theoretically able to practice a more open politics. The people would never elect an unreconstructed terror group, would they? After all, if all people had the same "universal values," that would include the Palestinians living in Gaza. When Hamas won decisively and began slaughtering dissidents, the Bush administration was shocked. They didn't understand that revenge, honor, religious piety, anti-Semitism, or militancy can be just as potent—or even more so—than Western notions of "freedom" or other material things.

After taking office in 2009, the Obama administration simply built on the prior White House's key philosophical insight, so-called, "universal values," and crafted policy that followed it to its logical conclusion. Where Bush was rightly suspicious of anti-American states, Obama embraced them. Where Bush had mostly ignored Muslim Brotherhood Islamist groups—believing them to be unpopular with Muslims and irrelevant—Obama correctly understood their attractiveness in the Middle East and backed them to the hilt against the Arab regimes which had long been America's regional allies.

So, for eight years, the Obama White House had downgraded its longstanding alliances with monarchies like Saudi Arabia and the United Arab Emirates while it prioritized relations with these countries' adversary in Iran and embraced the Islamic Republic's regional allies, Turkey and Qatar, as key interlocutors and partners. It did this for two reasons. First, because the administration believed that anti-Western, anti-American Islamism was the authentic political expression of the region.

The Obama administration also supported Islamist movements in the Middle East, principally the Brotherhood, that threated to topple regimes and instigate more hostility toward Israel. Countries which embrace political Islam and anti-Americanism, like Turkey, Qatar and Iran, were seen as relatively sympathetic warriors against a western global hegemon—virtuous forces of "resistance," without the usual alleged vices of imperialism, capitalism, Islamophobia, and so on.

Under any reasonable view of America's national or strategic interests, though, Qatar poses a threat to the United States and our allies in the Middle East, mostly owing to that country's enthusiasm for fueling Islamist groups like the Muslim Brotherhood. That source of danger for us is, paradoxically, what draws many on the political Left into Qatar's corner. Based on media coverage and opinion writing over the last several years, it's increasingly clear that the left-leaning mainstream media supports the Brotherhood; these activists, journalists and columnists seem to defend its patrons in Doha almost as an afterthought.

DESIGNATED HEROES AND VILLAINS

For many, the Left's support for the Muslim Brotherhood is a perplexing phenomenon. How could an alliance form between retrograde Islamic theocrats and social justice warriors? Don't their points of divergence—especially on social or sexual morality—make cooperation or support impossible? While these questions have been asked and answered articulately at book-length by David Horwitz[8] and Andy McCarthy,[9] the question is worth addressing here, if only briefly.

The Brotherhood fills a Leftist's need for an Islamist group that is "authentic" in its anti-American, anti-Zionist and anti-Imperialist sentiments. Its ideologues have come under fire for decades (not altogether unfairly) from true Salafists for being crypto-Marxist/Leninists and cultists.[10] In fact, there is considerable doctrinal overlap between the Muslim Brotherhood and the current incarnation of the Left, even if they're approaching one another from different directions.

Most consumers of news understand that the media, in general, plays favorites. It cheers on and protects its own Designated Heroes; it is with seemingly boundless energy, though, that the media relishes every opportunity to assail its Designated Villains.

We've long known, from polling[11] and other quantifiable metrics, that journalists have their own very pronounced political biases.[12] Even as journalists often indignantly tout the objectivity of their own work product and defend the credibility of others in their profession, the sorry results stand for themselves.[13] It's no longer controversial—other than in the most surreal, eye-rolling conversations with committed left-wing partisans—that the American media leans overwhelmingly left and has a strong preference for Democrats rather than Republicans.

The last decade of the left's radicalization, though, has seen the return of media's foreign Designated Heroes and Villains.[14] During the Cold War, left-leaning journalists, like their fellow ideologues on the political left, expressed their sympathies toward communist countries in a variety of ways, from the ostentatious pro-Soviet reporting of the New York Times,[15] to the cheering of communist revolutions or uprisings in places like Cuba,[16] Nicaragua,[17] the Palestinian territories,[18] and so many more.

In the most classic case, the media, together with fellow-traveler celebrities like Ernest Hemingway in the Abe Lincoln Brigade,[19] organized a campaign to provide inspiring, heroic (and thoroughly misleading) coverage of the left's gallant and romantic "freedom fighters" in the Spanish Civil War.[20] Evan as the military effort failed, the cause continues to be legendary in popular myth;[21] the successful communications strategy employed by the left's partisans became the blueprint for subsequent decades of agitprop for foreign leftist revolutions and communist insurgents. The occurrence and re-occurrence of this dynamic was so predictable, it was already being lampooned in Woody Allen's 1971 comedy "Bananas."

At the same time, of course, journalists now have foreign enemy states that are very much Designated Villains. The media treats these countries like it treats Republican candidates for office before a close election. All pretense of objectivity is discarded, and no amount of negative media coverage is enough to satiate the desires of reporters, editors and cable news hosts to wage total war.

The media's Designated Villains, then as now, are enemies of the political Left. What that means today—aside from Vladimir Putin and Russia which, thanks to a three-year campaign of media "collusion" frenzy, is in a category all its own—is relentless attacks on conservative or nationalist movements in Hungary, Brazil, Poland, Israel, the United Kingdom and the United States. Each of these movements are pro-American, stand against leftist transnational mores and are broadly sympathetic to Donald Trump's "Make America Great Again" program. While the particulars in each case differ, that's more than enough to make them the media's Designated Villains.

When we think of domestic political stories with Designated Heroes and Villains, it seems like a straightforward case of supply and demand for the political junkie and consumer of news. Republicans demand negative stories about Democrats because it confirms their biases and re-commits them to their ideological positions; Democrats demand the same stories of Republican malfeasance, corruption and evil. This kind of echo chamber, whatever its negative effects on the body politic is, nevertheless, comfortable.

But these foreign Designated Villains and Heroes are different. In nearly all cases (aside from Israel, which has a broad base of support in the United States),[22] there isn't a demand the supply of news coverage seeks to fill. The American public doesn't have strong feelings about a foreign country until the media reports on events or conditions there. Naturally, because of language and travel barriers, few Americans can experience or verify the reporting about a country half-way around the world.

What the public does know about these places and the leaders who govern them is almost exclusively a reflection on what they're hearing in the media. This, of course, makes journalists and editors remarkably powerful shapers of public opinion on American foreign relations—

and, in a time when their pretense of objectivity is abandoned so wantonly—they can be remarkably dangerous to our national security.

In a phenomenon common to each of the media's new foreign Designated Villains, the media sees itself less as factfinders chronicling and relaying information about current events, and more like participants in a morality play, complete with starring roles.

DONALD TRUMP IN THE NEW MIDDLE EAST

Even before taking office in early 2017, it was clear that the Trump administration would reverse the policies of his predecessor in the Middle East. When Donald Trump announced that his first trip abroad as president in 2017 would take him to Saudi Arabia and to Israel, it was a signal that the new administration had returned America's traditional alliances in the region to their privileged status.

Obviously, some were alarmed both at the American turn back to Jerusalem and Riyadh as well as the Trump administration's recognition of the threat of political Islam,[23] but none more than the architects of Obama foreign policy and the many talking heads, reporters, think tank wags and politicians who supported it and comprised their "echo chamber."[24]

That effort, spearheaded by former National Security Council Communications Director Ben Rhodes, organized a chorus of voices in support of Obama national security policy and waged brutal rhetorical war on its enemies in the press. Indeed, over the last decade, this community has come to broadly view the Iranian regime, Erdogan's Turkey and Qatar-sponsored Muslim Brotherhood as positive forces in the Middle East. Moreover, they resented the efforts by Israel and Saudi Arabia to combat their signature achievement, the Iran Deal, an agreement they believed would solidify a new alliance with that country.

Certainly, the Islamist conception of religion and politics is alien to this country's founding. It's aims, too, are contrary to the legal and ethical framework under which we have been governed for more than two centuries. If realized, the Brotherhood's agenda is, and continues to be, a clear threat.[25]

Nearly two decades after al Qaeda's 9/11 attacks on the United States, however, Ilhan Omar and Rashida Tlaib sit in Congress. They are among the most celebrated politicians in a radicalized Democratic Party, feted by a mainstream media that protects them (as well as it can) from scandal. The youthful energy of the American Left embraces the retrograde and anti-American positions of Islamists outside of political office, too, like Linda Sarsour. Correspondingly, those who create and distribute information or analysis about the threat posed by the Brotherhood are met with social media deplatforming, targeted media campaigns and other social and economic sanctions.

For these partisans, Donald Trump's relationship with Saudi Arabia—and Jared Kushner's reportedly close relationship[26] with the young anti-Islamist reformer Crown Prince Mohamed Bin Salman[27]—went a long way in setting the Kingdom as the next target for the hyper-partisan media: a Designated Villain. Like Israel's Bibi Netanyahu, MBS is so hated by the press, he might as well be a Republican.

Pro-American allied states like Saudi Arabia, Egypt and the United Arab Emirates draw these journalists' ire as they more forcefully take a stand against political Islam in general, and the Muslim Brotherhood in particular. All three Arab countries have, in recent years, banned the Brotherhood. Bin Salman called the group, an "incubator for all terrorists."[28]

Saudi Arabia and the United Arab Emirates have been locked in a bitter diplomatic and economic row with Qatar since 2017, when a coalition of anti-Islamist countries in the Gulf demanded Qatar cease its problematic behavior.[29] The coalition's 13 demands centered around Qatar's promotion of the Muslim Brotherhood and Iran, specifically mentioning the Islamist emirates information operations and use of their Al Jazeera network to foment dissent and revolution in the region.[30]

Arab leaders have been sounding the alarm about Qatar and the Brotherhood for some time. A 2009 cable published by WikiLeaks reports the Emirates' Crown Prince had strong words for US diplomats and the then-new Obama administration. What the Crown Prince didn't know, however, was that his American interlocutors didn't share his assessment of the dangers of Qatar; the passage of time would reveal both Obama's desire to strike a deal with Iran, and its promotion of the Brotherhood' "movement" in the region.

> On the margins of Abu Dhabi's largest defense exhibition (IDEX), Abu Dhabi Crown Prince Mohammed bin Zayed (MbZ) engaged visiting US dignitaries with strident remarks about Iran and Qatar's dangerous ties to extremist elements (including Iran and the Muslim Brotherhood). He stated flatly that Qatar is allied with the Brotherhood (posited as the UAEG's mortal enemy)... MbZ cited his own desire to defend his country as a counterpoint to extremists' loyalty to their "movement" as opposed to their constituent population.[31]

MbZ's criticism, as related by the cable's author, focuses on the Brotherhood as (1) an "extremist element" and (2) points to the group as a domestic seditious threat to the UAE, emphasizing the group's fealty to the "movement" as distinct from—and incompatible with—the laws that govern the state. Interestingly, this doesn't differ very much from typical American or European analysis of the threat of the Muslim Brotherhood.

The UAE even has gone as far as recognizing the Brotherhood roots of US-based Islamist groups like CAIR and Islamic Relief and designating them under their anti-terrorism provisions on the sound basis that they constitute the Brotherhood's powerful propaganda mechanism.[32] As all Islamists are keenly aware, these are significantly more aggressive steps against the Brotherhood than the United States or any non-Muslim country has taken—or, for that matter, has even contemplated—and form the basis of a near-hysterical hatred for which Islamist activists and politicians hold these countries globally.[33]

But no country is hated more by Islamists and the left today than Saudi Arabia, the richest and most powerful of the Arab anti-Islamist states—at least, as evidenced by the sheer number of relentless tweets about the country from the Brotherhood's favorite[34] new Member of Congress, Rep. Ilan Omar.[35] The avalanche of anti-Saudi media coverage in the mainstream press, however, reached a crescendo in the wake of the killing of Brotherhood-sympathetic Washington Post columnist Jamal Khashoggi late last year, and has been building ever since.[36]

Having found a Designated Villain in Saudi Arabia and its Crown Prince, the media drove a massive public relations effort to ostracize and punish Saudi Arabia economically, politically and (with regard to undermining its defensive war in neighboring Yemen against Iran-backed Houthi insurgents) militarily as well.[37] Reporters contacted companies[38] and entertainers[39] doing business in Saudi Arabia and demanded[40] they cease and condemn Saudi actions. Lobbyists with contracts with the Kingdom were harassed by, among others, journalists at the Daily Beast,[41] who threatened them with media exposure and shaming for legally working to make the Saudis' case to the American public.

Meanwhile, in Qatar, the Brotherhood—and its many offshoots including, most prominently, Hamas—flourishes[42] with official state support[43] and prestige.[44] It would take a tremendous effort, including large sums of money, to obscure these facts in the United States. This is one thing the Qataris don't lack.

Whether more experienced journalists would have been immune to the efforts of Qatar's lobbyists is an open question, but there's no doubt that the ferociousness of much of the reporting was influenced by the Trump administration's strong support for the anti-Islamist posture of Arab states like Egypt and Saudi Arabia,[45] and strong antipathy for the Islamist groups Qatar funds, harbors and promotes.[46]

Unable to resist the temptation to ideologically signal to its readers, the media transformed a serious Middle East national security issue into a simple morality play with the president and his allies, as ever, playing the part of the heavies. In this way, the vehemence of the media's anti-Trump hysteria aligned with Qatar's interests.

QATAR, THE ISLAMIST EMIRATE

Qatar occupies a small desert peninsula on the west of the Arabian Gulf and has one of the world's largest reserves of petroleum and natural gas. At less than 5000 square miles, the country is not much larger than the state of Connecticut.[47] While Qatar has neither the massive territory nor the easy access to oil that makes for inexpensive production in neighboring Saudi Arabia, the country's geographic location—not to mention its central place in the world's most coveted waterway—gives it great wealth and power. It is one of the richest countries in the world, based on per capita Gross Domestic Product, ranking between fifth and seventh in 2015 and 2016 data from the United Nations,[48] the International Monetary Fund and the World Bank.

Petroleum and gas account for 70% of its total government revenue, estimated at more than $191 billion in 2019 alone.

Using its wealth, Qatar has built a modern, cosmopolitan capital city on its eastern shore. While it was founded in the 1820s, Doha has emerged as the nation's most populous area. The Qatari state has spent lavishly on museums, urban infrastructure and planned communities that, no doubt, impress visitors from all over the world. The country's explosive growth as an international hub—with corresponding clout—tracks with the development of its Qatar Airways. The airline, established in just 1993 in Doha, now services over 150 international destinations with its fleet of over 200 aircraft.[49]

Like many other states in the region, though, Qatar owes its success and position to geological chance more than to the unique habits, traditions, achievements and other characteristics of its culture or citizenry.

In fact, Qatar isn't merely tiny geographically. Its total population of under 3 million consists primarily of imported foreign workers.[50] While none of these foreigners are integrated into Qatari society or granted citizenship, some are well-compensated consultants or other professionals who maintain the economic viability of the Qatari state.[51] Some others—the primary subject of this book—comprise a large class of imported Islamist intellectuals, terror group leaders and their shadowy financiers. Then there is an army of domestic workers, servants of Qatari citizens or other professionals from abroad.[52] The vast majority of the country's foreign workers, however, are common laborers, most of whom are forced live in conditions condemned by international human rights groups and investigative journalists.[53]

No more than 10-20% of the population are Qatari citizens. Online Qatar explains:

> Qataris are considered a 'minority' in their own nation with only 15% of them accounting for Qatar's total population. The remaining 88%

is made up of a workforce of over a hundred different nationalities. Qataris constitute only 10% of the country's total population, followed by other 13% Arab, 21.8% Indian, 7.35% Filipino, 12.5% Nepali, 12.5% Bangladeshis, 9.35% Egyptians and 4.35% Sri Lankan.[54]

It wasn't always this way. In 1951—even as Saudi Arabia was growing, thanks to the petroleum industry—less than 30,000 people lived in Qatar, and it was nothing more than a gulf-side backwater. Several decades later, thanks to continued oil exploration and the economic life it brings, the tiny nation was beginning to grow at a very rapid pace. 2007 saw the country's most dramatic growth rate—a 19% population increase.[55]

Of course, all of this growth is fueled by foreign workers who are never given the rights and privileges of Qatari citizenship. While these conditions ensure that there are more than enough servants for the rich, as well as professionals capable of keeping a society and government functioning, an underclass this size is a massive political liability for the Qatari state. The regime's precarious political stability is only ensured, then, by its continued economic success and growth.

The global economic downturn in the wake of the coronavirus pandemic is stressing all the economies in the Middle East, especially the dramatically falling demand for the energy that keeps so many countries afloat. Like its neighbors, Qatar largely locked down the country due to virus fears. While an extended lockdown might be tedious for the very wealthy, who live on large compounds or in lavish Doha apartments, nearly 90% of the country isn't so lucky. For the thousands of foreign laborers who live in cramped conditions (often referred to a form of modern-day slavery), an extended lockdown is less attractive and tenable. As the Guardian reports, "Qatar's migrant workers beg for food as Covid-19 infections rise":

> Low-wage migrant workers in Qatar, one of the richest countries in the world, say they have been forced to beg for food as the economic

fallout of the coronavirus pandemic takes a devastating toll, following a surge in the outbreak that has seen one-in-four people test positive.

In more than 20 interviews, workers in the World Cup host nation have described a mounting sense of desperation, frustration and fear. Many told the Guardian they have suddenly been left jobless, with no other way to earn a living. Others say they are desperate, but unable, to return home. Some have been forced to plead for food from their employers or charities.[56]

Even as this situation points to Qatar's vulnerability to civil discontent, the possibility of regime-changing revolution in Qatar is unlikely. Most of the foreign laborers are, probably, uninterested in revolution; as non-Qataris from all over the world—mostly Indian and southeast Asian—are separated from their families abroad, they have little stake in the country's future. Unlike in Europe or elsewhere, these migrant workers have been prevented from putting down roots. In the event of serious upheaval, more than likely, these laborers would return to their respective countries rather than work to create a new political entity in Qatar.

THE WAHHABBIS AND THE IKHWANIS

Throughout history, successful small nations survive and thrive by deftly leveraging their relationships with their larger, great power neighbors. In his books on the Cold War, historian John Lewis Gaddis has written convincingly about these smaller countries acting, in many ways, as the tail that wags the geopolitical dog; while under the protection of their more powerful sponsors or allies, small states can afford to be more outgoing or chance-taking in their foreign policy.[57]

This is certainly the case when it comes to Qatar. The al-Thani family came to power in Qatar in 1825, and is comprised of four main branches: Bani Ahmed, Bani Jaber, Bani Qassim, and Bani Thamer.[58] The clan has, until today, and maintained control of the small, peripheral territory through alliance with western nations for security and Islamic religious movements for religious legitimacy. The first source of religious authority for Qatar would be the Wahhabism on which the country is still established.

The movement was founded by Muhammad ibn Abd al-Wahhab, who lived in the Arabian Peninsula in the eighteenth century (1703-1792). He left his small, desert town to study Hanbali jurisprudence, first in Medina and then in Iraq and Iran. Upon his return home—not unlike Sayid Qutb—Wahhab was quick to condemn what he viewed as modernist corruptions of Islam then-present in the Arabian Peninsula.[59]

Like the Muslim Brotherhood several centuries later, Wahhabism was intended as an Islamic revival movement, starting from the assumption that a return to the pure fundamentals of the religion was necessary. Deviations in Islam since the time of Mohammed had produced decadence and dishonor, and Wahhabis looked to the past for a more "authentic" interpretation. For example, more than 100 years after Mohammed's death, some tribes continued to violate strict Islamic rules of idolatry, venerating rocks and trees. He was especially offended by the practices of the Twelver Shia, who venerated the life and tombs of holy men like saints. Wahhab developed a following but, it was only through an alliance with Muhammad ibn Saud in 1744 that the movement that bore his name, "Wahhabism" would grow in influence throughout the region. Saud would come to conquer much of the peninsula, eventually extending Wahhabism into Qatar.[60]

At first, the Wahhabis gave the ruling al-Thani clan religious legitimacy. In the latter half of the 20th Century, though, the Qatari royal family turned to the Muslim Brotherhood to provide a similar legitimating function.

Oil was discovered in Qatar in 1939 but, because of the Second World War, it took another decade until the country had built enough infrastructure to put its first barrels on the market.[61] It wasn't long before the fortunes of the tiny peninsula would explode into great riches, and the clout that only comes from a near-limitless ability to pull handfuls of money from the sand.

Shocked by its sudden wealth, the al-Thani family set about making Qatar a prominent part of the Islamic world. As Sunni Muslim rulers in the Middle East, they aimed to use orthodox Islamic tradition to buttress their claim to legitimacy and prestige. But the Qataris, quite reasonably, felt inferior to their neighbors and their Sunni cousins: Mecca and Medina were the two holiest cities in Islam; Cairo was the intellectual capital of the Arab world; Baghdad had a tradition of scholarship and jurisprudence that went back 1000 years. What did Qatar have, to show that it was something more than just an outpost for a nouveau riche Arabian tribe? Not very much. Qatar would have to use its money to build prestige in the Islamic world and it turned to one of the world's most formidable ideological movements for this support and legitimacy, the Muslim Brotherhood.

Much has been written on the Muslim Brotherhood from a doctrinal perspective. Superficially, it is an Islamic revivalist movement, looking specifically to the first generation of Muslims during the time of Mohammed. The Brotherhood was founded in 1928, as a direct response to the fall of the Ottoman Caliphate. Since that time, its members have primarily been concerned with restoring the Islam of the Caliphate. On a very basic level, that means government following the dictates of Islamic Law, or Shariah.

But that doesn't mean they are Salafis. The Brotherhood—or Ikhwan, as it's known in Arabic—was always less concerned about a return to specific doctrine than it has been concerned about the strategy and methodology that would, they believe, ensure such a return.

Very much like the first generation of Muslims, modern Muslims, they believed, weren't equipped to immerse themselves in the Qur'anic lifestyle without going through phases of readiness. They had to "prepare" for this change, to use a word associated with Brotherhood methodology.

Brotherhood figures were also concerned with how to apply the Islamic system of government to a modern, technocratic state. In the East, they looked to the competing systems of government that were, at the time, fighting one other in the West—liberal democracy, fascism and communism. These radical intellectuals wanted to borrow from each system and put it through an Islamic lens. They understood that the Ottoman Caliphate was not successful; it had been beaten by Western powers after 600 years. While they hated the freedom of the West, they also acknowledged that the Muslim world lagged behind the West—and the Islamists decided it was because their own governments and monarchies were decadent and un-Islamic. The Ottomans, they believed, did not take Islam or Shariah seriously enough.

So the systems of government they came up with would be more centered on Islamic law. They stole elements of fascism and communism as examples for how to build a modern state: big, imposing bureaucracies that keep their people in line through fear and total control. This appealed to them. They also looked to the Soviet Union and saw how it was possible to have an ideological state, where political enemies were punished in the service of that ideology.

Of course, the Brotherhood has kept terrorist violence—or the threat of such violence—within its doctrinal toolkit, maintaining close ties to other sympathetic terror groups. As the 9/11 Commission reported,[62] the Brotherhood's comfortable association with violent jihadist terror stretches from establishing clandestine "Special Apparatus" terror cells in the 1930s[63]—which are still active[64]—to the deep influence of Brotherhood ideologue Sayyid Qutb upon al-Qaeda.

The Brotherhood also constitutes the ideological wellspring for nearly every current jihadist organization. As al-Qaradawi notes in *Islamic Education and Hassan al-Banna*, it was the Muslim Brotherhood that "invigorated and promoted a view of Jihad that had lain dormant." "The movement of *Ikhwanul Muslimoon* (The Muslim Brothers) breathed new life into jihad," he wrote. "Giving it a place of honor and prominence in writings; stressing its importance in lectures, meetings, and songs; and asserting its sovereignty over individual and collective life."[65] Where al-Banna provided inspiration and organization, Sayyid Qutb provided the roadmap. His 1964 book, *Milestones* operationalized a plan for the reestablishment of totalitarian Islamic law through a skillful mixture of indoctrination and physical violence, all pegged to long-established concepts in Islamic law.[66]

Interestingly, the Brotherhood's arrival and settlement in Qatar coincided with the group's far better-known arrival in Europe and the United States. In all these cases, the Muslim Brotherhood was used to lend Islamic religious and ideological legitimacy to the Muslim community in their new host nations. Every country had a slightly different reason for turning to the Brotherhood when they exploded from Egypt in the late 1950s and early 60s.

After Egyptian president Gamal Abdel Nasser's crackdown on its senior leadership in that decade, the Muslim Brotherhood was decimated. While prominent figures filled Egypt's prisons and torture chambers, the Brotherhood's younger generation wasn't yet important enough to face Nasser's wrath. Too junior to face imprisonment, they had a stark choice: either walk away from the Islamist cult, or flee the country.

Some left the Brotherhood, but those who were especially committed to the cause escaped to regroup elsewhere. In *A Mosque in Munich*, Ian Johnson traces the Brotherhood's arrival in Europe and their relatively quick rise to assume the leadership of organized Islamic life on that continent. In the middle of the Cold War, the Central Intelligence Agency, too, played its familiar role of embracing the perceived "moderate" Islamists and, naturally, funding them to the hilt.[67]

The Brotherhood was part of a Western plan to use the Soviet's restive Muslim minority as a weapon against it. The Soviet Union had outlawed the practice of religion, including Islam. In fact, nearly half of the USSR's 15 republics had a Muslim majority: Azerbaijan, Kazakhstan, Kirghizia, Tajikistan, Turkmenistan, and Uzbekistan. Given the attachment many of these people feel for Islam, canny analysts and politicians in Washington believed that traditional American conception of freedom to practice one's religion publicly could be used to contrast with Soviet materialism.[68] Muslim Brothers attacking the treatment of Muslims in the USSR would be used as counterpropaganda against the Soviets' offensive information operations targeting African Americans in the United States and highlighting America's own legacy of racism and slavery. In order for this to work, the Brotherhood, then, would have to be helped into a position of Islamic authority in the West—especially in Europe—and the establishment of Brotherhood-led infrastructure like Mosques and community centers was encouraged, even clandestinely funded by Western intelligence agencies.

Of course, they came to America, as well. Like the Muslim Brothers who arrived in Europe, most of them would be university age. In contrast to many of the uneducated Egyptians who comprised that country's Salafist groups, the younger Brothers came seeking degrees and middle-class professions in their adopted home.

It's important to remember that Americans have largely been miseducated about the enemy we've been fighting since 9/11. Our conception of "Islamic radicals" or "radical Islamists" or "extremists" more appropriately describes the unwashed, bearded, mountain- and training camp-dwelling Taliban fighters we faced in Afghanistan. These are the most backwoods and simpleminded of Islamists. Muslim Brothers aren't any of those things, and never have been. Mohammed Morsi's life is a good example. He and his wife joined and became active in the Ikhwan while he was a graduate student in the United States, at the University of Southern California. He joined the local chapter of the Muslim Students Association, a long time Brotherhood front.

Morsi emerged victorious in the 2012 election that put the Brotherhood's political arm—named, for gullible western consumption, the Freedom and Justice Party—into power. Like so many Brothers, he was a trained engineer. The secretive group has benefitted greatly from the massive cadre of engineers, doctors and other professionals in its ranks; they understand how systems work. The Brotherhood has been chiefly concerned with building infrastructure to support its vision of Islam, creating the institutions to reinforce Brotherhood ideology from birth until death.

These students would go on to establish the associations that would come to comprise America's new Muslim community around the college and university towns where they lived and studied. The Muslim Student Association was the first of many groups.[69] The MSA has grown to nearly 600 chapters on college campuses in the United States and Canada. "Through conferences and events, publications, websites and other activities," the Investigative Project on Terrorism reports, the "MSA has disseminated and promoted militant Islamic ideologies on college and university campuses throughout North America."

When the Muslim Brothers built this infrastructure in America, it hadn't existed before. While Europe had long had a small, postwar population of mostly Turkish Muslims, the university towns where the

Brothers settled in the United States had never seen mosques, halal groceries or meat-markets. And, owing to the American tradition of religious tolerance, they were able to create outposts here without much resistance from their surrounding communities or competition from other strands of Islamic doctrine or observance. Outside of largely non-Arabic-speaking African American converts, the Muslim Brothers were free to create the structures of Islamic life in this country from scratch.

It's important to remember that the constellation of groups that comprise America's Islamic institutions are a product of the Muslim Brotherhood's diligent efforts. Had non-Islamist Muslims emigrated to the United States in large numbers—or had the Brotherhood never fled from Egypt—the contours of the US Muslim communality could look very different. On the other hand, non-Islamists were less likely (and less motivated) to create these institutions and initiate such a massive, multi-generational effort. In this case, fortune favors those who think about "community organizing" and amassing institutional power—and the Brotherhood has always been focused on that, to the exclusion of nearly everything else.

As that first generation of Muslim Brothers in the United States would age and mature, they'd go on to create an infrastructure that roughly corresponded with their needs. After the student groups, they would create would a support system for Islamist professionals, and then a pedagogical mechanism for families. Around the late 1970s, this generation began to be increasingly concerned with education. They devised programs with which to educate their children in Brotherhood doctrine, and Tarabiya Guides and other Islamist youth programs became popular.[70] With a community established, they looked to spread Islam and proselytize to non-Muslims, building interfaith outreach mechanisms and publishing manuals like *Methodology of Dawah*.[71]

They are engaged in this building process in every country in which they operate—in non-Muslim and Muslim and societies, as well. Unlike in the West, Egypt, Saudi Arabia and the United Arab Emirates now recognize that the Brotherhood's parallel institutions are a threat, not just as an engine-room of jihadist radicalization, but anti-government subversion, as well.

The most important theoretical work from the Brotherhood's prominent ideologues and its top American think tank, the Virginia-based International Institute of Islamic Thought (IIIT), involves figuring out how to exist in the modern world while adhering to Brotherhood's conception of Islamic principles.[72]

These principles are totalitarian, but they're also pragmatic: while they consider achieving an Islamic society the goal, their pragmatic awareness of Muslims' minority status in places like the United States makes it necessary to build alliances. In America, the most fruitful alliance is with the political Left.

There's significant overlap between the two when it comes to political outcomes. In *Social Justice in Islam*, the Brotherhood's most potent ideologue, Said Qutb, conceptualized how to make the massive, 20th Century administrative state work for a government bureaucracy in the service of Islamic values.[73] More recently, Qatar-based Yusuf al-Qaradawi has devoted his considerable influence to prevent westernization and integration of Muslim minorities into the non-Muslim countries where they reside.

In Qatar, however, the Muslim Brotherhood was not swimming against the tide of an alien culture. In the 1960s, it was an Islamic country, but it was small, nearly empty outpost on the edge of the desert. The Brotherhood would be responsible for building, among other things, the educational infrastructure that would, its leaders hoped, turn the backwater of Doha into an important capital of Islamic learning and thought.

Qatar's most promising recruit was Yusuf al-Qaradawi, a brilliant and charismatic Egyptian student who fled to Qatar at a time when many younger Brotherhood figures were finding new homes across the world. Once things settled down in Egypt, Qaradawi was able to return, Qatari passport in hand, to graduate from Cairo's Faculty of Theology at al-Azhar University in 1973 with a doctorate in Islamic jurisprudence. Qaradawi's dissertation focused on *zakat* (obligatory charity) in Islam and, while at school, he was a well-known leader of several Muslim Brotherhood student groups. Upon completion of his doctorate, Qaradawi returned to Doha to use the al-Thani family's largess to build Qatar into the capital of Islamist ideology.[74]

The Brotherhood, too, had its own very good reasons to embrace the Qataris. While it was, at the highest levels of its leadership, a cult-like secret society, the Brotherhood had managed to grow its base of support in Egypt into the millions. It had built newspapers, publishing houses, and a relatively robust local infrastructure of activists and supporters throughout the country. These are tremendously important assets to any political or religious movement, and they're not to be abandoned lightly. If the Brotherhood could, at a future date, seize power on a large scale in any nation, it would almost certainly be in Egypt, the most important and populous Arab country.

That said, Egypt was dangerous for the Brotherhood; with the great potential rewards came the tightrope walk of coups, crackdowns, and imprisonment. By the late 1960s, the group had already been through several crackdowns by the Egyptian government, and it would be a fear that would hang over the Brotherhood's ambitions for decades more until the present day.[75] Qaradawi and the Muslim Brothers who followed him to Qatar in the first few decades were hoping that the tiny Gulf emirate would be a place where the Brotherhood would have a secure home. It was a wise bet. For the Brotherhood, Qatar turned out to be a lot more than just a refuge.

Ensconced in Doha, Qaradawi set out to work. Harvard's Religious Literacy Project describes his major impact on the direction of Qatar's religious institutions, beginning with a flurry of activity as soon as he moved back from Egypt, degree in hand.[76]

> [Qaradawi] moved to Qatar in 1961 to lead an institute of religious studies and quickly established himself as a popular preacher. He became a personal guide to Sheikh Khalifa al-Thani, who granted him a Qatari passport after Egyptian authorities refused to extend his stay in Qatar. This allowed him to travel and lecture widely. He served as the principle of the Religious Institute (ma'had dini) beginning in 1961 and founded Qatar University's Faculty of Shari'a, which began accepting students in 1977. In 1973 he became the director of the Islamic Studies Department at Qatar University's College of Education, and in 1980 founded the Centre for Sunna and Sira Studies, also at Qatar University. In 2008, the Emir's wife, Sheikha Mozah bint Nasser opened the al-Qaradawi Research Center for Islamic Moderation and Renewal at the Qatar Foundation's Faculty of Islamic Studies.

Since Qatar's most prominent export—the state-owned television network Al-Jazeera—was founded in 1996, the Brotherhood has played a crucial role in programming and setting the editorial line, providing the network's strong ideologically Islamist backing.

Qatar's vast petro-wealth enabled Qaradawi to become the world's most prominent Sunni Islamic authority. He was given a call-in television show on Al-Jazeera called, "Sharia and Life." That show made him an international star, bringing Qaradawi into living rooms all across the Arabic-speaking world.[77] In 2000, the network estimated a nightly viewership of 35 million, and "Sharia and Life" was among its most popular programs. Qaradawi would dispense his view of Islamic jurisprudence to callers, answering their question about matters both religious and political. This high-profile platform won the Brotherhood many more sympathizers and allowed the group to spread his message.

It also caught the eye of the Brotherhood's critics, especially in the West, and unsurprisingly, Qaradawi became embroiled in several controversies. In a perfect illustration of the contrast between Western attitudes toward Islamists and the view currently prevailing in the Gulf, Harvard Divinity School lauds Qaradawi as a "moderate," just as Saudi Arabia's Arab News recently described Qaradawi as, "the hate preacher who became Doha's spiritual guide"[78]

"Like Qaradawi, other Muslim Brotherhood members have been drawn to Qatar as a friendly space where they can meet and disseminate ideas without risk, compared to the hostile political climate in Egypt. Qaradawi has often played a role in organizing Brotherhood meetings in Doha."

In explaining why Qatar can never turn its back on the Brotherhood or anti-western Islamism, scholar David Warren stressed the importance of the Islamist cleric and his legacy in that country. "The Qatari royal family became a key supporter of Qaradawi," he wrote.[79] Today, Qaradawi meets regularly with the emir and Qatar's royal family; and, as a signal to Islamists across the globe, the state media distributes photos of the royal family embracing the sheik with great affection and reverence.[80]

THE ENGLISH AND THE AMERICANS

Since the ruling al-Thani family assumed power, Qatar has managed to align itself with powers that buttressed its position and fortunes both ideologically and militarily. Qatar used its central geographic location within the Arabian Gulf to entice the English, the preeminent naval power of the day, into an alliance.

The 1868 affirmation of the British government's Perpetual Maritime Truce of 1853 between Bahrain, Qatar and Abu Dhabi was the first formal recognition of Qatar by a western power.[81] As the Ottoman Empire unwound, it relinquished its claim to Qatar in 1913. Three years later, the al-Thani family would again seek regional security from the British, becoming an informal British protectorate under the trucial system until Qatar's independence in 1971.[82]

In exchange for protection against regional adversaries, the Qataris allowed the English to build a port, and a forward operating base for their navy as it maintained the free flow of commerce through the Straits of Hormuz. In exchange for influence over Qatar's foreign policy, the British helped the al-Thanis put down threats to their rule from competing local tribes or regional powers. Throughout history, small kingdoms and countries have found this kind of arrangement profitable.

Prior to the 9/11 attacks, al-Qaeda and Bin Laden demanded that "crusader" armies—meaning, the United States—withdraw its military from the Arabian Peninsula.[83] Through its longtime alliance with America, they maintained, Saudi Arabia wasn't only bringing dishonor to the Islamic ummah; it was violating key tenants of Islamic jurisprudence as it relates to foreign policy. For the Muslim Saudi monarchy to invite non-Muslim American troops to fight against Muslim Iraqi soldiers during the first Gulf War, and then stationing troops on the territory where Mohammed lived, was a serious violation of Islamic law.[84]

In an attempt to placate this Islamist grievance, in 2003, the United States withdrew its forces from Saudi soil. But the second Gulf War against Iraq was already in motion, and there was never any serious consideration of withdrawing from the region entirely. Smaller states in the region stepped up and offered their territory for the US military. [85] For these countries—Oman, Kuwait, the United Arab Emirates and Qatar—the American military presence was a massive gift: not only did it cement the security of the ruling regime, it gave these countries an increasing amount of soft-power leverage over the United States, as we'll see in the case of Qatar in particular.

While it has been in use since the 1990s, following the US military's exodus from Saudi Arabia's Prince Sultan Air Base, Qatar's al-Udeid Air Base grew to be the largest base in the Middle East.[86] Today it houses bout 10,000 service personnel. It is the home to the US Combined Air Operations Center, US Air Forces Central Command, US Special Operations Command Central Forward, and CENTCOM Forward HQ.[87] Naturally, Qatar's vast wealth make their stay in the country a comfortable one.

For many US policymakers, Qatar's efforts to subvert the US relationship with a newly anti-Islamist Saudi Arabia—as well as its promotion and funding of Islamism abroad—must always compete with the utility of having access to the al-Udeid Air Base. As long as the US military advocates on behalf of the base's continued use in that country, nearly any amount of trouble and mischief Qatar creates will be accepted, excused or contextualized. Far from being an American strategic asset in the Arabian Gulf, al-Udeid is, in fact, a Qatari asset in Washington.

Thanks to the U.S. military presence at the al-Udeid Air Base, Qatar's grip on the constellation of national security professionals in Washington is nearly total. Rather than being a strategic advantage for this country, the base allows Doha to extort the United States. Cracking down on Qatari support for terrorism is always weighted against the massive and very real logistical issues involved with abandoning the base.[88] It's easier, they've found, just to look away.

Amid the row with Saudi Arabia and the UAE over Qatar's funding of terrorism in 2017, former Defense Secretary James Mattis had only warm words for the emirate.[89] The same year, Anne Patterson, the controversial former U.S. Ambassador to Egypt under the Obama administration[90]—whose good relations with Islamists in the Muslim Brotherhood scandalized Cairo and made her the most hated woman in Egypt—was mercifully passed over for a top job in the Pentagon.[91] It's unsurprising, considering her history, that Patterson landed at the US-Qatar Business Council.[92]

For the Saudis, the US military's withdrawal to its neighbors' territory solved a regional public relations problem that its longtime enemy, Shia Iran, had exploited. Without being used as an American military base, the Kingdom wouldn't appear so much like a puppet or junior partner to an infidel power. At the same time, however, the Saudis would come to greatly regret this shift in the balance of power. It was the first step towards allowing the eventual degrading—and then possible replacement and repudiation—of an alliance that had survived decades, from the end of World War II through the Cold War, Middle East wars, oil embargos, 9/11 terror attacks and more.

The American shift away from Saudi Arabia began in 2003 and, ever since, Qatar has aggressively tried to offer itself as a strategic replacement. On the positive side of the leger, it has spent lavishly on cultural projects, and cynically funded educational institutions, as well. At the same time, Qatar has also stoked resentment against its rival.[93] Despite Khalid Sheik Mohammed's links to the Qatari government,[94] Saudi Arabia, rightly, was the focus of much of the blame for the emergence of al-Qaeda and the 9/11 attacks in the United States. Qatar has taken advantage of this—as well as the long history of draconian punishments and religious persecution in Saudi Arabia—in a wide-ranging information operation against the Kingdom in this country.

THE ANATOMY OF INFORMATION OPERATIONS

Information operations use media and traditional tools of public relations to advance policy interests through narratives. They take place primarily within the confines of public discourse, using mass media to disseminate weaponized information. It is weaponized, meaning, it leads one to a conclusion about the topic at hand.

In an information operation, the consumer or the target is given information with which he will determine a course of action. In basic scope, information operations are campaigns of mass influence like any other, not unlike a shoe company would undertake to sell more sneakers. That shoe company is providing prospective customers, on a large scale, with public information about their product which will lead them to making the decision to purchase their product. In electoral politics, this kind of campaign is undertaken to convince a citizen to cast a vote for a particular party, and to shun another. In public affairs, a campaign would be undertaken to agitate for a policy change—either stoking public pressure on policymakers to make the change, or directly targeting the policymakers themselves.

In today's media environment, that information might be in the form of news articles on websites, newspapers and magazines; commentary on blogs, in podcasts or on YouTube; or in television segments on cable news broadcasts. What distinguishes the information operation from other influence efforts, however, is the basis in reported news; these are wars waged primarily using the raw materials provided by the media. Reporters provide the ammunition, and then a chorus of voices move the weaponized information through the public. Sometimes this process is staged, pay-for-play, or the result of bribery; often they're not. This effort forms part of a campaign and is in contrast to or complimentary with traditional advertising. It is used because it appears to be organic and genuine and, in many cases, it comes pretty close.

In his several books, Edward Bernays—known as the father of modern public relations—recounts the contours of several dozens of successful campaigns. In fact, his books are filled with examples of ingenious displays of intellectual problem-solving from the position of an expert practitioner. It's striking that, even as Bernays' *Crystalizing Public Opinion* was published in 1923 and draws from examples from the very first years of the 20th Century, the basic elements have not changed very much, if at all. [95]One particular anecdote stands out today. While this campaign was instigated by a media outlet in service of making more money by increasing its advertising rates, the tactic used—to increase the magazine's influence and clout, including a change in public policy—makes it startlingly similar to a modern information operation.

> A nationally known magazine was ambitious to increase its prestige among a more influential group of advertisers. It had never made any effort to reach this public except through its own circulation. The consultant who was retained by the magazine quickly discovered that much valuable editorial material appearing in the magazine was allowed to go to waste. Features of interest to thousands of potential readers were never called to their attention unless they happened accidentally to be readers of the magazine.
>
> The public relations counsel showed how to extend the field of their appeal. He chose for his first work **an extremely interesting article by a well-known physician,** written about the interesting thesis that "the pace that kills" is the slow, deadly dull routine pace and not the pace of life under high pressure, based on work which interests and excites. **The consultant arranged to have the thesis of the article made the basis of an inquiry among business and professional men throughout the country** by another physician associated with a medical journal. Hundreds of members of "the quality public," as they are known to advertisers, had their attention focused on the article, and

the magazine which the consultant was engaged in counseling on its public relations.

The answers from these leading men of the country were collated, analyzed, and the resulting abstract furnished gratuitously to newspapers, magazines and class journals, which published them widely. Organizations of business and professional men reprinted the symposium by the thousands and distributed it free of charge, doing so because the material contained in the symposium was of great interest. A distinguished visitor from abroad, Lord Leverhulme, became interested in the question while in this country and made the magazine and the article the basis of an address before a large and influential conference in England. Nationally and internationally the magazine was called to the attention of a public which had, up to that time, considered it perhaps a publication of no serious social significance.

Still working with the same magazine, the publicity consultant advised it how to widen its influence with another public on quite a different issue. He took as his subject an article by Sir Philip Gibbs, "The Madonna of the Hungry Child," dealing with the famine situation in Europe and the necessity for its prompt alleviation. The article was **brought to the attention of Herbert Hoover**. Mr. Hoover was so impressed by the article that he **sent the magazine a letter of commendation** for publishing it. He also **sent a copy of the article to members of his relief committees throughout the country**. The latter, in turn, used the article to obtain support and contributions for relief work. Thus, while an important humanitarian project was being materially assisted, the magazine in question was adding to its own influence and standing.

Now, the interesting thing about this work is that whereas the public relations counsel added nothing to the contents of the magazine, which had for years been publishing material of this nature, he did make its importance felt and appreciated. [Emphasis added.]

The emphasized sections above are the heart of the campaign. Even more than 100 years ago, most of the elements of today's political warfare are apparent, including: the use of basic building blocks of information (the all-important magazine articles); the targeting of influencers as an important audience (described as "the quality public"); the organization of expert voices and talking heads (the symposium and Lord Leverhulme's speech); and, finally, a political figure taking concrete action (Hoover).

Looking more closely at Hoover's role makes the comparison to today even more apparent. At the time these events took place, he was not yet the President of the United States (he'd serve from 1929-1933, being elected some six years before the book was published), but he was certainly no stranger to public life and the political world. He served as the Secretary of Commerce under Presidents Harding and Coolidge and, before that, as Woodrow Wilson's Director of the US Food Administration. There's no indication in the text that Hoover was involved in the operation; he seemed to be so taken with the narrative promoted by the magazine's campaign, he gave them a letter of commendation.

The magazine Bernays described used Hoover's action as legitimating and clout-building; it would burnish the magazine's reputation as essential reading. It would make it the kind of magazine people who change policy feel they should be attentive to, with the commensurately high advertising rates that match that kind of audience. In a modern information operation, however, that resulting action from Hoover would be the end in itself. Other than that intention, though, the outline is essentially the same.

Looking at the campaign, something else is important—but it's written between the lines. Not one of these things happened organically; even as the anecdote obscured the operators' machinations behind the scenes in passive voice, you can be sure that they kept pressing the momentum of the campaign forward. For example, it was not by happenstance that articles, "were collated, analyzed, and the resulting abstract furnished gratuitously to newspapers, magazines and class journals." Lord Leverhulme, the "distinguished visitor from abroad," was enticed to take the campaign's narrative before a large, influential audience in a speech. Presumably, someone did the enticing, and using methods that are left to the reader's imagination—from simple curiosity and naïve interest to any manner of corruption.

While Bernays and his work have come to play a dark role in conspiracy theories over the last several decades, there's nothing especially cynical or malevolent about his techniques. At a very basic level, someone persuading you in any way holds some kind of power over you, even if you arrive at the conclusion independently. The task of the persuader is to change your mind about something or, if he doesn't have to go through the trouble of persuading you—if you're already in agreement—he must cement or strengthen this belief or opinion.

The point at which persuasion becomes manipulation is an interesting question. Bernays himself painted it in perhaps the worst possible light in his 1928 follow-up book, *Propaganda*:

> The conscious and intelligent manipulation of the organized habits and opinions of the masses is an important element in democratic society. Those who manipulate this unseen mechanism of society constitute an invisible government which is the true ruling power of our country. We are governed, our minds are molded, our tastes formed, and our ideas suggested, largely by men we have never heard of.... It is they who pull the wires that control the public mind.[96]

When a friend tries to convince us to buy the new kitchen appliance they've fallen in love with, we're listening friendly advice. When a company or spokesperson makes the same pitch through omnipresent, nagging, and targeted web advertising, though, we are more circumspect, because they stand to gain financially from the effort. But an exchange of money on its own doesn't necessarily mean we're being swindled; sometimes that kitchen appliance does indeed make our lives better and is worth the money.

At first glance, then, it appears that the use of dishonest information or techniques which include dishonest testimony, like paying off talking heads, would be the difference between an honest campaign and a dishonest one.

In politics, however, the question gets more complicated—especially when it comes to campaigns that promote a party or ideology. Strongly held political ideas are among the most powerful motivators; being a part of an information operation that advances one's ideology can be its own reward, just as appealing as financial or reputational renumeration. In contrast to traditional public relations campaigns or advertising, ideological commitment plays an instrumental role in all political information operations, including both the anti-Trump Russia Hoax as well as Qatar's efforts in this battlespace. This fervor inspires freelance activists, social media provocateurs and journalists to dive into the effort, on both offense and defense.

For example, in 2016, chatter about "information warfare" and "influence operations" was everywhere. In no time, Democrats and the media began to scream about treason and subversion. Their vocabularies suddenly swelled with terms of art from the world of intelligence, and they gravely affected a deep knowledge of foreign nations' clandestine activities in the United States. The jargon and vocabulary associated with these things—including, of course, obvious Russian transliterations of English words like, "kompromat" and "dizinformatzia"—appeared knowingly on the lips of TV talking heads and in feverish Twitter threads.[97]

It was a media frenzy at full tilt; over the next several years, the intensity would ebb and flow, but the media would make sure it would never recede from public view. The ubiquity of the narrative, though, could sometimes disguise the amazing feat of rhetorical acrobatics involved. When the mainstream media jumped, head-first and with great enthusiasm, into a conspiracy theory alleging all manner of

Russian influence on America's political system, it was reversing itself after a full century of dismissing the threat of subversion.

Of course, this entire narrative was a cynically concocted hoax. For years, everything that a regular consumer of mainstream, left-leaning news and cultural products would think he knows about Donald Trump and Russia would be a lie. While it warned darkly of manipulations of the press, in halls of power and on social media, this Russia Hoax was, itself, a textbook example of an information operation.

A negative message is always more potent than a positive one, so operators of all kinds quickly find that the easiest way to advance one's interests is to coordinate and weaponize media attacks on one's enemies or rivals. In politics, the narratives are often crafted to be as wide as possible, which leads practitioners of political warfare to be tempted to be as comprehensive or as scorched earth as possible toward their enemies. Sure, they're focused on a single election—but the effort put into a robust information operation would, hopefully, reap rewards for longer than just one season. For example, the Russia Hoax was hatched to prevent Donald Trump's election in 2016; Democrats used the same narrative to score congressional victories in 2018. They tried to launch a variation of the Russia Hoax—the Ukraine Hoax—in early 2020, which culminated in an unsuccessful impeachment trial in the House of Representatives.

Now, the existence of this campaign itself—or, to be sure, the use of aggressive information operations—indicates little about the relative merit of the product, candidate or cause. The tools and basic techniques themselves are relatively value-neutral; this is simply how large numbers of people are communicated with and swayed in modern societies.

And the presence of foreign actors alone doesn't necessarily indicate skullduggery or deception, either. In open societies like ours, there's nothing wrong with a foreign ally presenting its point of view to the

American public or to policymakers; indeed, there's nothing inherently wrong with the use of traditional tools of public affairs or information operations by anyone. It's a free country, and our Constitution's (maybe, by this point, theoretical) guarantee of free speech enables the expression of a variety of points of view.

In other words, when everything is on the level—meaning, of course, that it isn't built on and advanced through the use of faked documents or questionable evidence or pushed by an ideologically committed or financially compromised media—the information operation could be considered a part of the give-and-take of the political conversation. It is, for better or for worse, how the deliberative process works in America.

LESSONS FROM THE HOAX

In 2020, America is significantly more jaded and cynical than it was in Bernays' time more than a century ago. And yet, several recent developments in media have made the country's political life far more susceptible to hostile information operations. First, reporters and editors abandoned dispassionate reporting—even the veneer or pretense of objectivity—in favor of furthering ideological causes. Then, after the collapse of the media's traditional print advertising-based economic model, reporters began to rely almost exclusively on private, for-hire opposition research shops to generate their content. "Experts" transitioned from those with subject matter expertise to those who could make a splash on cable news.

This book will address each of these changes in turn. As perhaps the most successful information operation in modern times, the contours of Russia Hoax contains many lessons for us when examining similar techniques of and dynamics present in Qatar's efforts in the United States.

The first lesson is the rapid pace of an information operation's effectiveness and saturation. A narrative can grip the partisan imagination with terrifying speed—even if that narrative contradicts a century's worth of political and cultural messaging. Even more importantly, a truly comprehensive effort has the power to shift public perception on even the most important of issues. Millions of Democrat voters can go from decades of waving peace symbols to unbelievable belligerence against Russia in months, or even weeks. By the same token, Qatari information operations targeting rival Saudi Arabia have been able to weaken and shake a powerful alliance with the United States that has persisted through more significant trials. Why the US-Saudi relationship us under more stress today than following the 9/11 attacks is due in whole part to the offensive Qatari information campaign waged against it.

Secondly, we know that, for the instigators of these information operations—whether it's the Russia Hoax's Fusion GPS or Qatar's army of lobbyists, media operators and diplomats—it's always a matter of money. These are professionals, hired for their expertise and their connections to reporters and editors. The journalists who run with their stories and narratives, however, are not often directly compensated by the client; their reward comes in two forms. Larger platforms and bigger paydays await media figures who get the good scoop, have deep sources, and generate clicks or viewers.

But that's not to say that today's media would jump on any story or any narrative that's of journalistic value or one that would guarantee attention and wide exposure. The other piece of the puzzle is ideological commitment—and, for nearly everyone in the American mainstream media at any level, the obligation to protect the narratives and heroes of the political Left supersedes much else. They have come to see themselves as not as impartial chroniclers of events or even muckrakers on a mission to drain political life of corruption; they are now political actors, doing their job to advance the cause of an ideology.

The final stage of a political information operation is action when it comes to policy. This is not to say that campaigns would be considered unsuccessful if they simply change perceptions and convince large numbers of people.

Qatar is successful in its information operations in the United States for the same reason that the Russia Hoax was so easily sold to mainstream journalists, administrative state functionaries, and think tankers: because the targets were already the Designated Villains of the Left, these people wanted desperately to believe it was true.

THE MEDIA'S COLLAPSE AND REBIRTH AS 'ECHO CHAMBER'

Media outlets were once more circumspect about the ethics of, say, splashing the purloined contents of hacked documents or weaponized information on their front pages. They were once uncomfortable with using leaks from unscrupulous information operators and media fixers. How the media got there is a story worth exploring.

Thanks to decades of Hollywood mythmaking, the image of the forthright, fearless and dogged journalist has been cemented into our consciousness. We imagine reporters are hardworking and dedicated to the public interest, more-literate gumshoes pouring over evidence like Elliott Ness, trying to get to the truth and report it to the public. Films like "All the President's Men" (1976) or "His Girl Friday" (1940) Sam Fuller's "Park Row" (1952) advance a heroic, crusading image of the profession. Even more cynical pictures, like "Ace in the

Hole" (1951) or "Citizen Kane" (1941) show the journalist as hypercompetent and intelligent, if dastardly.

In many ways, this image wasn't entirely false. Journalism was once something like a blue-collar profession; it was, at the very least, working class.[98] The impression of grizzled and street-smart reporters and editors with highly functional bullshit detectors wasn't merely a fantasy of motion pictures. A century ago, a reporter was likely a combat veteran, especially after the GI Bill of 1944.[99]

Then they had their regular beats—meaning, specialty subject areas they would cover over time. In that way, young reporters, faced with the daunting task of assimilating complex subjects and explaining them to their lay readers, gradually became real experts. "Compared with reporters who consider themselves generalists, beat reporters develop a deep understanding of the context of new scientific findings within a specific area," writes freelance journalist Knvul Sheikh.[100] "This contextual knowledge sharpens their ability to judge when a new finding is newsworthy and when it's simply a small step in the field."

Five, 10 or 20 years on the national security or local crime beats, for example, could provide more than enough expertise to challenge nearly anyone more credentialed. They could go toe-to-toe with their interview subjects or sources, rooting out rhetorical obfuscation and digging into scandals. Even if they had their prejudices—and, as thoughtful human beings, they no-doubt did—journalists at least had subject matter expertise and the willingness to call balls and strikes.

A free people, governed by a republic or a democracy or any combination of the two, depends on truthful (or, at least truth-adjacent) deliberations on major issues. The public, as well as the health of the public discourse, counts on the acuity of journalists' bullshit detectors. Over the course of the last two decades, though, the institutions performing this important societal function disappeared. What replaced it would bring cynicism, confusion, and make the country ripe for hostile information operations, both foreign and domestic.

When the Internet replaced the traditional print media in the late 1990s, the advertising revenue on which massive newsroom and research budgets depended plummeted. Over the next decade, media outlets were faced with a collapsing economic model and needed to cut costs in order to survive.[101] They could no longer able to afford to work months or even years on complex and important stories. They could no longer afford to keep their own foreign bureaus, and they could no longer afford to pay veteran reporters and editors with decades of experience, contacts, sources and, perhaps most importantly, discernment and judgement.[102] Many outlets folded completely or were subsumed into large conglomerates, becoming prestigious loss-leaders for entertainment companies, cable companies or, eventually, billionaire gadflies.[103] The surviving outlets—even those freed by their new patrons from the shackles of having to turn a profit—would still need to generate product.

At the same time, a younger generation of woke, unapologetically political journalists entered the workforce. As media companies have found their resources shrink, they found it more profitable to jettison some of the work from highly-paid, more experienced reporters and editors in favor of increasingly ideological woke clickbait generated from young staffers, listicles, and fulsome explorations of things like the "internet culture" beat.[104] The importance of agitating for political priorities and enforcing new cultural standards blinded many in the industry to the reality of their failing business model.

If there was some regret about turning over American journalism to a younger generation in the country's newsrooms and board rooms, it wasn't often expressed. Not only were these cheaper young workers more economically attractive to newly broke media outlets, many of them very quickly seemed to have remarkable sources and access to the White House. This wasn't an accident.

Ben Rhodes was the Deputy National Security Advisor for Strategic Communications in the Obama administration. Once an aspiring short story writer, Rhodes rose to prominence within a particular subset of the Democratic foreign policy establishment. He spent five years working for longtime Indiana Democratic Congressman Lee Hamilton and, from that perch, was a primary contributor to the 2006 report of the Iraq Study Group, co-chaired by Hamilton and former Secretary of State James Baker.

By 2008, Rhodes was working as a speechwriter for then-candidate Barak Obama. By all accounts, the partnership was fruitful from the start; they shared a way of looking at the world and had ideas about how to fix its problems. Obama and Rhodes sought ambitiously to realign the Middle East and, especially, the role of the United States within it.[105] Obama recognized his staffer's gift for narrative—but Rhodes' genius was in building, sustaining and rewarding a powerful army of journalists who'd enable him to shape that narrative.[106]

Rhodes cynically recognized that, by judiciously handing out exclusives, leaks and scoops, he could build young reporters into famous, well-paid and loyal activist journalists. Most importantly, access to the White House would ensure that these new stars would be supportive of Rhodes, his party, and his administration. Even putting aside the young journalists' ideological commitment to the Democratic Party, its politicians and woke, liberal ideology, the material rewards that came with playing along were substantial: sizeable salaries, constant television exposure, Pulitzer prizes, massive Twitter followings and—more enticing than anything else, perhaps—the entrée into the 'smart set' of establishment political life in Washington.

This is a credentialing process, a factory—and a win-win for all the players involved. Even Rhodes understood that he was dealing with blank slates. As he explained to the *New York Times Magazine*'s Dave Samuels in the final months of the Obama administration, "The average reporter we talk to is 27 years old, and their only reporting experience consists of being around political campaigns… They literally know nothing."[107]

What they did understand, Rhodes found, was fervent ideological and partisan commitment. He discovered it relatively easy to influence a press corps of young liberal reporters who viewed themselves more as partisan "agents of change" than of dispassionate journalists.

"When the foreign and national bureaus were closed, [young reporters] didn't know it wasn't OK to be a journalist and a political operative at the same time," Lee Smith wrote of this problem in 2017. "They thought it made them more valuable, even patriotic, to put themselves in the service of a historic [Obama] presidency. And they'd replaced for pennies on the dollar all the adults who could have taught them otherwise."[108] These journalists—as well as the young editors they'd increasingly be reporting to—would believe what Rhodes tells them, and they would frame their stories from his point of view.

To the extent that many of those in the media industry noticed their dropping readership and the growing hostility of many Americans to their political hectoring, the media began to view dissenting customers as literal counterrevolutionaries to be pushed from civic life. "The last mass trials were a great success," Greta Garbo's Ninotchka intoned, with dramatic, Soviet earnestness in Ernst Lubitsch's 1939 film. "There are going to be fewer, but better Russians." And so it goes, too, with the dwindling number of the media's consumers.

As more and more journalists face unemployment, media partisans have sought to blame corporate consolidation and the changes brought to the industry by the crisis of cratering advertising revenue. Of course, there's a strong element of self-serving denial in this analysis; it's far easier to blame the usual capitalist bugaboo than to face the prospect that, for too many years, news consumers thought their product was partisan rubbish.

AMERICAN MEDIA IN THE SERVICE OF QATAR

Mehdi Hasan seems to be everywhere on TV. [109] [110] [111] Following the terrible 2017 terror attack on two mosques that left nearly 50 dead in New Zealand, cable news outlets couldn't seem to get enough of this very articulate man with an English accent who spits fire against Donald Trump and rails against Islamophobia and Israel. Reliably Trump-obsessed cable channels like CNN and MSNBC relished the opportunity to promote a foreign-born Muslim guest who, they believe, has the credibility to call the president and his supporters racists and white supremacists. And Hasan, for his part, relished both the spotlight and the opportunity to make his case directly to a sympathetic, hysterically anti-Trump audience in the United States.

After spending the last several years claiming to be concerned about Russia interfering in American politics, though, it's a bit jarring to see the employee of a state-run media outlet hostile to the United States appear so frequently on American mainstream media. By promoting Hasan, these cable news outlets are facilitating the mainlining of foreign propaganda. At the time, Hasan worked for al Jazeera; when appearing in American media, he was no less a government spokesman than Kellyanne Conway or Kayleigh McEnany. [112]

What these networks are doing is unwittingly participating in an information operation that "launders" the credibility and reach of an agent of influence like Hasan to millions of unsuspecting American viewers. It works like this: Because CNN or MSNBC's Trump-hating viewers agree with Hasan's anti-Trump message, they'll soon come to see him as a credible source on other issues, as well.

The al Jazeera host's near-nightly presence on cable news represented an alarming example of how Qatar uses the infrastructure of American partisan politics and media to advance its interests, but it's only one of many. Despite being a relatively unstable country—where a whopping 88% of the population is comprised of foreign laborers—Qatar's vast wealth can alter policy by manipulating narratives and perceptions using weaponized information in the form of news, opinion and influential voices like Mehdi Hasan's.

When, in 2019, Mohammed Morsi died of a heart attack while appearing in an Egyptian court, the news of the former Muslim Brotherhood leader's demise lit up the most committed parts of the Qatar influence network.[113] This was especially true for the Islamist terror groups that depend on Doha for their survival.[114] The Islamist regimes in Turkey, Malaysia and Qatar were the only countries to publicly react to Morsi's death, with warm tributes from Qatari emir Tamim bin Hamad al Thani,[115] Turkish President Erdogan,[116] and Foreign Minister Saifuddin Abdullah of Malaysia.[117]

Despite absurd claims that the emirate has no special relationship with the Muslim Brotherhood, Qatar's state-run al Jazeera covered Mori's career and death with heroic zeal.[118] Scanning through the network's massive Tweet thread and 11 news and analysis pieces that day, it's clear, though unsurprising, that the Brotherhood leader was undergoing a beatification in Qatar's global media mouthpiece.[119] Lamenting the comparative lack of response to the death from all non-Islamist world leaders, al Jazeera complained that, "the reaction has been largely muted in many capitals."

Soon after the news broke, though, it was time for anguished cries from the Left. As we will see, both Qatar and the Muslim Brotherhood have positioned themselves as natural allies of the Left. Not only do they all share an anti-western, anti-imperialist outlook, but Qatari messaging in English has lately featured anti-capitalist themes, as well—especially on al Jazeera, AJ+ and its series of Doha Debates. So it's no surprise that, following Morsi's death, Twitter and the mainstream media filled with tributes to "the first democratically elected president of Egypt," with the deceased leader and the Brotherhood serving their usual roles as avatars for democracy in the Islamic world. There was, also, fist-shaking rage at Egypt's current president Abdel Fattah el-Sisi. And throughout, there was plenty of revisionist history from left-wing Brotherhood-supporters in the press and at left-leaning 'human rights' groups.

Some in the Arab media took note, and a few reactions from anti-Islamist Muslims in the region have been fantastically deadpan. "Across the world," the website Cairo-based Egyptian Streets news site reports, "reactions [to Morsi's death] also came in from *a number of organizations and groups including Human Rights Watch, Hamas, and the Muslim Brotherhood.*"[120]

Taking their cues from Islamists, outlets and activists on the Left like Human Rights Watch tell their own, slanted story about the Brotherhood's short-lived rise to power in Egypt. As many of the group's critics (myself included) had predicted, Morsi slaughtered democracy in Egypt not long after he and his party assumed power. Towards the end of his first few months in office 2012, Morsi issued a controversial declaration, effectively ending the "democracy" the Left had cheered in the election,

"The president may take the necessary actions and measures to protect the country and the goals of the revolution," the declaration read.

It also placed Morsi above the law, stating the president can "claim exception against all rules."[121]

For the last five years, pro-Islamist media, activist and 'human rights' groups have wrongly painted Morsi's removal from office as a "coup." Morsi's thugishness while in power—as well as the public's disgust at the Brotherhood's corruption and economic mismanagement—caused an estimated 14 million Egyptians (in a country of 84 million) to rise up in 2013 and support the military's removal of Morsi and his government. Despite a lot of negative press from Islamist supporters in the media, it's rarely acknowledged that the massive protests that swept Morsi from power were among the most well attended anti-regime protests in modern world history.[122]

"If only Mohammed Morsi was a journalist," a *Washington Post* columnist might say to herself. "There's so much we could do with this." In reviewing that paper's coverage of the deceased Muslim Brotherhood president, it's inescapable to conclude that the paper would feel comfortable re-living some of the magic of its hysterical coverage of political operative-cum-journalist Jamal Khashoggi: so much high dudgeon, self-righteousness and thirst for vengeance against Saudi Arabia.[123]

The *Washington Post's* shameless promotion of Islamists on its pages disserves its own, more fulsome examination going back at least a decade. It's editorial board has written many times in opposition[124] to a wildly popular bill from Texas Senator Ted Cruz to classify the Muslim Brotherhood as a terrorist organization.[125] Islamists are rarely, if ever, given critical treatment in the Beltway's hometown paper; their narratives are always embraced and amplified They're treated to far better press than a conservative or a Republican would get.

Not long ago, Wael Haddara was given space on its pages to echo its own editorial board's condemnation of the Sisi regime and special pleading for the Muslim Brotherhood.[126] [127] Haddara is the former president of the Muslim Association of Canada and a veteran of several other Hamas- and Brotherhood-affiliated Islamist groups, including the Muslim Association of Canada and CAIR's Canadian branch.[128] In 2012, Haddara was so taken by the prospect of Brotherhood rule in Egypt, he traveled there and became a close advisor of Morsi's, doing communications work and selling the group's narrative to credulous westerners.

The Post has even given its pages over to Islamists more (openly) bloodthirsty than the Muslim Brotherhood. In November 2018, the Post published a piece by the head of the Supreme Revolutionary Committee of the Iran-sponsored Houthi insurgency in Yemen, Mohammed Ali al-Houthi, declaring that he and his terror group, "want peace for Yemen."[129] While Jeff Bezos' outlet assures us that "democracy dies in darkness," the Post's readers are not informed about the relative sincerity of the Houthi leader's plea, considering its slogan remains, "Allah is the Greatest. Death to America. Death to Israel. Curse on the Jews. Victory to Islam."[130] Of course, very little of this is ever mentioned in outlets like *the Washington Post*; it would complicate the bold, simple colors in the painting they're struggling to create.

The Saudi Foreign Ministry didn't acknowledge Morsi's death, but cheekily tweeted an infographic warning of the threat of the Muslim Brotherhood.[131] The image—dramatically splattered with blood—echoes what Crown Prince Mohammed bin Salman has long said about the Islamist group, that it "does not represent Islam and affects the stability of societies."[132] True enough. It was inevitable that, as Islamic countries in the Middle East more confidently embraced a new, pro-American nationalism, they would become the media's Designated Villains.

The Intercept is an investigative site founded in 2014 that describes what it does as, "adversarial journalism" and is supported financially by eBay founder and Pierre Omidyar, funder of several anti-Trump non-profits.¹³³ The site began as a platform from which to weaponize the documents released by Edward Snowden but has since shifted its primary focus to the Middle East. In that region, outlet's adversaries are, primarily, the traditional structure of America's alliances, especially Israel, Saudi Arabia and the United Arab Emirates.

While national security and foreign policy is *The Intercept*'s main focus—and its greatest information warfare victories have been in that space—the site has begun to branch out to cover other social justice issues in the United States, as well. Its most prominent public face is editor Glenn Greenwald, fervently anti-Israel journalist-activist and former Salon and Guardian columnist best known for his work with Snowden and as a harsh critic of US foreign policy.¹³⁴

After covering the leaked NSA documents, *the Intercept*'s next prominent story was the first shot in an offensive, weaponized campaign to end surveillance or law enforcement scrutiny of the Muslim Brotherhood in America. In "Meet the Muslim-American Leaders the FBI And NSA Have Been Spying On," Greenwald and former Guardian and Al Jazeera reporter Murtaza Hussain created a massive, 8700-word impassioned defense not only of the Muslim Brotherhood's privacy rights, but for the fundraising mechanisms for the designated terrorist group, Hamas, as well.¹³⁵

The piece was remarkably well-written and based on documents and internal leaks from members of the intelligence community and the Obama administration—officials from which were doubtless instrumental in crafting the article. At the time, the U.S. government was busy shutting down terror prosecutions, preventing law enforcement and homeland security agents from learning about Islamism by censoring subject matter training, and restricting what could be said about the Brotherhood and political Islam.

Needing an excuse to end a law enforcement effort undeniably meant to keep Americans safe, staffers in government almost certainly leaked the surveillance program's existence to *the Intercept* in order to justify taking action. The report was picked up by a staggering array of media allied with the Left, from the *New York Times* to *Rolling Stone, Lawfare, The New Yorker, Wired, US News & World Report* and a host of far-Left sites like *Democracy Now*. Soon the story was everywhere, and the government had the justification it needed to back off the Brotherhood and other domestic Islamists.

The campaign was aimed directly at changing US government policy with respect to interdicting terrorist activity in the United States, and it succeeded.

In the summer of 2017, the inter-GCC conflict between Saudi Arabia and the UAE against Qatar became a clash that generated worldwide media interest. In this conflict, *The Intercept* was emphatically in the Qatari camp. It is important to note that while *The Intercept* has political positions which align closely and unambiguously with Qatar (and, by extension, the Muslim Brotherhood and Turkey), there is very little coverage of the terror-supporting emirate in its pages. But it doesn't need to; propping up Qatar explicitly wouldn't sit comfortably alongside it mission of "adversarial journalism." Rather, *The Intercept* advances Qatar's interests by relentlessly attacking its enemies. And it succeeds by constantly drawing blood.

In the last few years, *the Intercept*'s pro-Qatar media coverage has been extensive, and several of its reporters have beats related to different offensives.

Interestingly, though, the country that generates the most negative coverage is the United Arab Emirates. Ryan Grim has written extensively on the Emirates and has appeared in media and in public events as a fierce critic of Sheikh Mohammed bin Zayed and his regime. The constant drumbeat of scandal has taken a severe toll on the UAE's reputation inside the Beltway and especially on the Left, where *The Intercept* is seen as credible journalism.

Thanks to the economics of the news business and social media, in today's media environment, even the largest, most well-financed outlets sacrifice investigative staffs and deep research in favor of using cost-free political operators like Fusion GPS and others. But these resources—provided free to journalists—don't necessarily have to be for-profit enterprises. It's probable that intelligence gathered by nation states like Qatar or Turkey finds its way into *The Intercept's* articles or generate the articles in the first place.

Critical to the site's success is that, while its editorial point of view is clear (and its Designated Heroes and Designated Villains are unambiguous to any reader), it nevertheless positions itself as an objective, sober outlet for investigative journalism. It does not position itself as an outlet of the Left, though it very much is an outlet on the far Left. That its "adversarial journalism" happens to target the same villains is left to the discerning reader.

QATAR'S OWN MEDIA ASSETS

Information warfare products consist of weaponized information that is translated into a variety of media—from books to articles, television interviews, blog posts, and tweets. Qatar's media empire encompasses 38 sports television channels in 36 countries, exclusive broadcasting rights to Turner-owned channels in the Middle East and North Africa, a Qatar Airways-sponsored monthly travel series on

CNN, and more.¹³⁶ "Qatar has quickly and quietly built an unrivaled global influence operation," says Brooke Goldstein, Executive Director of The Lawfare Project. "It presents a squeaky-clean face to the west that hides the regime's support for the most extreme Islamist groups… groups that murder Israelis and gravely threaten U.S. interests."

Founded in 1996, al Jazeera is the most important news network programing in Arabic in the world, with tens of millions of viewers spread across Arabic-speaking communities in nearly every country. It is a Qatari state-funded enterprise run by Hamad bin Thamer al-Thani, a trusted member of the royal family.

The tiny Gulf Emirate speaks the left's language; the narratives its state-run al Jazeera-English network promote dovetail perfectly with a social justice-focused audience in the United States. As we have seen, al Jazeera commentator Mehdi Hasan even rails against widespread "white supremacy" in America and Trump's alleged Islamophobia nightly on CNN, earning him and his network tremendous credibility and support from its left-wing viewers.¹³⁷ Qatar's ability to influence Beltway and media opinion in this country is a deep subject that deserves its own close examination.¹³⁸

Most Americans learned about al Jazeera after the 9/11 terror attacks. Many criticized the network for aiding in Islamist propaganda campaigns by rushing to air footage and messages it obtained from al Qaeda, the terror group behind the attack, which was delivered by courier. The network was attacked by then-Defense Secretary Donald Rumsfeld in 2003. "We know that Al-Jazeera has a pattern of playing Taliban propaganda over, and over, and over again," he said. "And they have a pattern of not making judgments about the accuracy of the propaganda. Is that unhelpful to us? You bet."¹³⁹

In 2017, former al Jazeera reporter Yosri Fouda claimed that Qatari royal family members—including the former emir, Sheikh Hamad bin Khalifa al Thani, met in secret with al Qaeda members in order to obtain the terror group's recorded messages the network would subsequently broadcast through the Arab world.[140] Fouda, who worked on broadcasts for al Jazeera in 2002, alleges that the Qatari government paid $1 million for a message from al Qaeda to commemorate the first anniversary of the 9/11 attacks.

"The fact that there is anti-Semitic material in al Jazeera is significant; that that it has a daily diet of anti-American material is significant," as former Middle East Broadcasting Network head Alberto Fernandez put it during a 2018 conference on Qatar's influence operations in Washington. "But the greatest problem with al Jazeera is how, for a generation, it has mainstreamed and normalized an Islamist grievance narrative, which has served as sort of the mother's milk for all sorts of Islamist movements."[141]

Drawing a massive estimated audience of 35 million weekly, al-Jazeera's most popular Arabic program was "Sharia and Life," starring Qatar-based virulently anti-Semitic cleric Yusuf al-Qaradawi, the prominent Muslim Brotherhood's jurist.[142] Qaradawi's most infamous statement was an ode to Adolf Hitler. "Throughout history, Allah has imposed upon the [Jews] people who would punish them for their corruption," he proclaimed on al Jazeera.

> The last punishment was carried out by Hitler. By means of all the things he did to them—even though they exaggerated this issue—he managed to put them in their place. This was divine punishment for them. Allah willing, the next time will be at the hands of the believers.[143]

As London-based Muslim liberal Nervana Mahmoud noted, the Qatari outlet, "labels Arab states with good relations with Israel [like the United Arab Emirates and, most recently, Saudi Arabia] as 'Arab Zionists.'"[144] Of course, this kind of rhetoric makes Middle East normalization and eventual peace and with Israel more difficult.

But the network is more than just a platform for Islamist propaganda; al Jazeera is the world's most successful and influential state-directed information operation. Its sophistication is evident in its ability to promote two very different messages to two audiences simultaneously. In Arabic, al Jazeera pushes a stream of vile, anti-Semitic conspiracy theories, and attempts to rile up religious and extremist Muslims against attempts at positive, human rights reforms in Egypt, Saudi Arabia, the Emirates and other Arab states.

In English, however, al Jazeera presents itself as progressive and left-wing, attacking these same nations efforts at reform as fake and inadequate. A re-branding in English as "AJ+" was further meant to obscure the Islamist-run network and to appeal to younger people in the West, with social media material in English, Arabic, French and Spanish.

An army of professional staffers, producers and minders make sure al Jazeera's mask is held tight, but occasionally it slips. In 2019, both AJ+ Arabic and al Jazeera itself were rocked by a severe anti-Semitism scandal, beginning with a Holocaust-denial video.[145] The video—professionally produced by the Doha-based network—denied that extermination took place at the Nazi concentration camps and accused the Zionist movement of benefitting from the atrocities. Soon, the network's critics were finding recent tweet after tweet from a variety of al Jazeera contributors.[146]

In an attempt to quell the anger that threatened to destroy all the effort al Jazeera had put into cultivating AJ+'s reputation and target audience, the network suspended two staffers. Calling the disciplined employees "scapegoats," Muslim liberal commentator Asra Nomani tweeted, "The government of Qatar needs to take responsibility & everyone making excuses for al Jazeera is complicit in a coverup."[147]

The scandal did do damage to Qatar's influence operation—but just how much damage is yet to be seen. At the very least, more Americans know that the AJ+ social media content that's targeted toward their children and young adults is actually al Jazeera, a foreign network owned and operated to advance the interests of the Qatari state. This kind of exposure is vital.

Unfortunately, many American elites and policymakers have long been soft targets for Qatari information warfare, especially if they're coated with the sheen of the network's respectability. Even Hillary Clinton gave the state-run Islamist network the highest praise. "Like it or hate it, [al Jazeera] is really effective," the then-Secretary of State told lawmakers on Capitol Hill in 2011. "It's real news."[148]

After the 2016 election, with the specter of comparatively tiny Russian news and commentary outlets like Russia Today and Sputnik blown out of perportion as serious threats to American democracy, the massive Qatari elephant in the room, al Jazeera, had largely escaped similar scrutiny. In recent years, thankfully, Congress finally appeared to be getting serious about foreign states' role in information operations directed at American citizens and media consumers. The 2019 National Defense Authorization Act requires all foreign media outlets based in the United States—including Russia's network Russia Today and Qatar's al Jazeera— to identify themselves clearly as foreign outlets and report to the FCC every six months on their relations with their foreign principals. To date, neither foreign outlet has filed with the FCC or made their report available to Congress.[149] Unless real penalties are levied against these networks, nothing much will change.

EXPERTS AND TALKING HEADS

Having a reporter frame the news in an advantageous way is nice— it's certainly more than any Republican has—but by 2009 Ben Rhodes understood that it's not comprehensive enough to be truly impactful as information warfare.

A typical news story or tv news segment might feature a journalist to report the news; it might reference a recent think tank study; and, finally, provide several experts to contextualize the importance of the news and provide historical perspective. What would happen to the coverage if all of these elements shared a common benefactor—especially one that is adamant about message discipline and advancing its interests?

Of course, spinning reporters and promoting experts isn't exactly new; it's been standard practice in political warfare since the birth of the first press corps. But building an army of newly credentialed "expert opinion," though, was new—and even more useful.

These new faces, from non-governmental organizations and think tanks, would soon appear all over media on the Obama White House's behalf, dutifully pushing their narratives. Their lack of real subject matter expertise would be compensated by their access to government; like the few remaining veteran journalists who were more skeptical, the older generation of experts would be shunned by the White House in favor of younger, more enthusiastic evangelists for Obama policy.

Soon the young activist journalists have quotes that look like independent confirmation of the White House line. Here's how Samuels describes the information warfare infrastructure Rhodes created during the Obama administration:

> In the spring of last year, legions of arms-control experts began popping up at think tanks and on social media, and then became key sources for hundreds of often-clueless reporters. 'We created an echo chamber,' [Rhodes] admitted, when I asked him to explain the onslaught of freshly minted experts cheerleading for the deal. 'They were saying things that validated what we had given them to say.'

One of the most important elements of an information operation consists of the use of credentialed voices. These people are essential in lending credibility to a narrative with the use of their title or professional background.

In March 2019, the New York Times published a breathless and expansive story in its Sunday magazine, arguing that Democratic support for Israel was quickly evaporating in the wake of an ascendant Boycott, Divestment and Sanctions (BDS) movement.[150]

Nathan Thrall, the piece's author, tried to make the case that prominent Democratic donors worked deviously behind the scenes to maintain public support for Israel, even as the party's base soured on the Jewish state. Thrall painted a bleak picture of Israeli atrocities and echoed age-old themes of untoward Jewish influence in America's paper of record. Yet, nowhere in the piece did the Times disclose that those paying Thrall's salary have an agenda deeply hostile to Israel. Shortly after the story's publication, it was revealed that Thrall's employer, the International Crisis Group (ICG), received about around $4 million—or 40 percent of its foreign funding—from the Emirate of Qatar, with other funding coming from notorious U.S.-based backers of BDS.[151]

We tend to think of foundations as kinds of non-partisan non-profits; the Qatar Foundation, however, is different. It exists to advance the priorities of the state. Even as it has been routinely criticized for promoting Islamic extremism, including anti-Semitism, the Qatar Foundation has been, since its inception, a way for the Emirate to project soft power—usually influence, in one way or another—in the service of its national interests.[152] In fact, the Foundation's three shareholders are the very highest echelon of Doha's royal family, the Emir of Qatar, Tamim bin Hamad al-Thani; his father, former Emir Hamad bin Khalifa al-Thani; and his father's consort, Moza bint Nasser.

More than any other nation, Qatar has shrewdly invested in the infrastructure of this kind of influence, and it shows. The Qatar Foundation also literally owns Brookings Center Doha,[153] the Qatar-based branch of one of the oldest think tanks in the world, the Brookings Institution. The Foundation's listed "100%" ownership stake means that the Brookings Center Doha is actually controlled by Qatari heads of state. Exposés in the New York Times[154] and at Tablet[155] in 2014 show that, rather than producing objective, data-driven analysis about the region, Qatar's millions colored the work the think tank produced. "[T]here was a no-go zone when it came to criticizing the Qatari government," said Saleem Ali, a former visiting fellow at the Brookings Center Doha, told the Times. "If a member of Congress is using the Brookings reports, they should be aware; they are not getting the full story."

In a pointed back-and-forth with Brookings' Strobe Talbot, writer Lee Smith addressed the glaring omissions in Brookings' coverage of the region:

> Many of those who follow developments in the Middle East, especially the Arab-Israeli peace process, would presumably be interested in some "objective, fact-based analysis" of why Qatar, ostensibly an American ally, hosts the head of a group that has killed Americans, and waged war against U.S. allies. Readers might also benefit from a hard look at other terror-sponsoring activities that Doha is widely reported—by the U.S. Treasury Department, among other credible sources—to engage in. But I can find no mention at all of Doha's close and comfy relationship with the head of a State Department-designated foreign terrorist operation anywhere on the Brookings site.[156]

And yet, members of the media and policymakers still use Brookings as an independent, authoritative source of analysis on the Middle East. That this continues to work—thanks to the biases of the media and others who don't want to look too closely at the sources of funding and influence—is both obscene and cynically impressive.

And yet, members of the media and policymakers still use these outlets as authoritative sources of analysis on the Middle East. Qatar-backed media outlets—including those, like CNN, that count on substantial advertising revenue from the oil-rich emirate—often feature talking heads from Brookings, ICG and other institutions with undisclosed financial ties to Doha.[157] This cynically impressive scheme continues to work, thanks to the biases of the media and others who don't want to look too closely at the sources of funding and influence.

For Qatar, endowments to Brookings and the International Crisis Group are tiny pieces of a much larger strategic influence campaign it has waged successfully in recent years, spanning from these multi-million-dollar investments in Washington think tanks, universities, and dozens of media outlets it owns globally; to, most recently, a controversial and hard-knuckled eight-figure lobbying effort in Washington.

Qatar also spends lavishly on universities, not only in the United States itself, but to create a network of American-affiliated schools in the emirate that will be predisposed to support it and its policies.[158] The Qatar Foundation paid six U.S. universities—Cornell, Texas A&M, Carnegie Mellon, Virginia Commonwealth University, Georgetown, and Northwestern—hundreds of millions of dollars to operate campuses at the Education City complex in Doha. These academic institutions are where you go to reach some of the most prominent and influential academics and, almost as an added bonus, you've got access to thousands of impressionable future targets of influence ops as well in the student body. Both professors and students make the implicit deal that, in order to live off Qatar's largesse, there are limits to the types of things that they can discuss.

OPPO SHOPS AND LOBBYISTS

Two interesting characteristics of journalism's recent decline are apparent in the wake of dramatic layoffs at BuzzFeed, Gannett, Yahoo, AOL, Vice, the Huffington Post and other online outlets.[159] The first is the industry's commitment to propagandizing for social justice politics in thousands of cheap, disposable clickbait articles. The other, in the more ostensibly serious reporting that's left, is the extent to which reporters and editors allow freelance influence operators and media manipulators to craft meta-narratives using their bylines and media outlets.

At the same time as activist journalists' content was being generated with great ideological fervor, much of the exhaustive investigative reporting produced by these media outlets' more experienced reporters was—from the dual necessities of the bottom-line and dwindling attention spans—largely outsourced to public relations shops, opposition research peddlers, or other political operators.

When both of these potent temptations collide, the resulting media products are nearly always so histrionic as to undermine the potential for serious reportage about America's political scene. What's left is essentially stage-managed conspiracy mongering delivered in a self-righteous, venomous and vindictive style.

A journalist's job had always entailed use of help from a variety of gray-area agents of influence who would be helpful in a variety of ways, from pitching a story to providing carefully selected experts to interview and more. However, this new media environment, with today's young reporters with little experience but ideological enthusiasm to spare, made reliance on these cynical political operators nearly ubiquitous. Given the woke politics of the press corps, and given the right target—that is, a conservative, Republican or anti-Islamist—it is remarkably easy for one of these operators to successfully bounce a story through the media, onto television news, to Congress and back again.

Nearly a decade ago, Glenn Simpson and Peter Fritsch found a far more lucrative gig than their previous work writing at editing at the *Wall Street Journal*. With a massive list of contacts to fellow journalists they'd amassed from years in the industry and their genuine skill in writing and research, they founded Fusion GPS, the gray-area media firm and public relations shop that would be an engine for hundreds of articles promoting wild conspiracy theories about Donald Trump and Russia. By any standard, Fusion GPS should be considered among the most successful information operators of the last century: the for nearly three years, the political media landscape has been a hall of mirrors that Simpson, Fritsch and his colleagues created.

In the Russia Hoax, Democratic operatives were paid to "dirty up" the reputation of then-candidate Donald Trump. In this case, the derogatory narrative would focus on Trump's supposed malevolent ties to Russia. In order to do so, a large mountain comprised of little bits of "evidence" would be put into the media; at some point, these small stories would pile up and create a narrative.

Paid operatives would build a narrative about Donald Trump, his family and his associates from opposition research. This research, in fact, was conjured up from thin air, or assembled from someone's half-baked theories or hearsay. They would peddle it, bit by bit, to the media, promising exclusive scoops and, with it, opportunities to appear on television and secure ever more lucrative contracts at more prestigious journalistic outlets.

In the special case of the Russia Hoax, the articles created using the operatives' research would reach a special audience—members of the US intelligence community—who could, by virtue of their position, take steps to credulously investigate the far-fetched claims. These investigations would yield the hoped-for leaks back to the press and, suddenly, the headlines blare that the highest levels of the national security bureaucracy are taking the accusations seriously.

This is precisely what happened (albeit in greatly simplified form) with the Steele Dossier, the opposition research document that, eventually, formed the basis of several multi-year investigations into Donald Trump and his associates. As always, the document (the "evidence," such as it purported to be) is the backbone of an information operation; it forms the raw material from which an over-arching political narrative is built.

Being able to pull off that hall of mirrors effect has been remarkably profitable. It's labor-intensive work, building on years of professional and personal relationships; only the most well-heeled of clients can afford to engage in this kind of political warfare at the very highest of levels.

Prior to the 2016 election, Fusion GPS' clients on their Russia stories included the Hillary Clinton campaign and unnamed supporters of several of Donald Trump's Republican primary opponents. If political campaigns have the resources to ensnare most of the media (and half the country) into a maelstrom of Russia conspiracy drama, surely a foreign nation with vast oil and natural gas wealth could underwrite such a campaign to destroy a single man's reputation in the service of its interests. But Fusion GPS isn't the only game in town when it comes to sleazy, journalism-corrupting influence operators; it's just among the most effective.

We've seen how Qatar's vast wealth can alter policy by carefully manipulating narratives and perceptions using weaponized information in the United States. Most of their most effective spending, though, isn't on well-heeled advertising and public relations firms like Ogilvy; Qatar has funded think tanks and media outlets that get them a much bigger bang-for-the buck.[160] In that way, they're able to shape the information battlefield— rather than simply replying to a story, owning or partnering with media outlets allow Qatar to create an environment that's favorable to their interests.

In Qatar's war against its enemies in the United States, the tiny Emirate had the help of a phalanx of grossly well-funded lobbyists. After the 2016 election, several lobbyists from Trumpworld unfortunately went to work for Qatar and have been the locus of most of the anti-Saudi activity in media and in Congress. Republican lobbyists like Stonington Strategies' Nick Muzin and Avenue Strategies' Stuart Jolly and Barry Bennett (at a jaw-dropping rate of $500,000 *per month*) relentlessly attack Qatar's enemies.[161]

The emirate undermines the stability of its Arab neighbors, especially Saudi Arabia and the United Arab Emirates; it promotes Islamists like the Muslim Brotherhood in vulnerable, Western open societies; and, finally, it diplomatically and financially supports violent terrorist groups like Hamas, which have threatened Israel daily.

Of course, nobody who can credibly called pro-Israel would like to be in the position to defend these policy priorities, even for satchels of cash on offer from Doha. Nevertheless, after Donald Trump's shocking victory in the 2016 election, two well-connected Jews became lobbyists and signed a substantial contract to represent the Islamist-supporting emirate of Qatar in the Arabian Gulf. That decision would get them working against Israel's interests and, eventually, do considerable damage to their careers and reputations.

Modern information warfare is slick and unnoticeable; influence operations, though, are as seedy as they look. We understand that, when politicians or influencers are taken on lavish, all-expense-paid junkets, it's a clear example of bribery. The quid pro quo[162] (say, on a trip to the Doha Forum) doesn't have to be immediate, and it doesn't have to be readily apparent; there is, however, a promise of some kind of profit: money, fame, career advancement, or even virtuousness.[163]

Wealthy nations like Qatar have the ability to extend these kinds of benefits to a great many people, and they do.

An influence operation is the strategic use of interpersonal relationships and institutions. A long-term relationship or affiliation with an institution or person builds and solidifies the kind of good-will that can be immensely valuable for a lobbyist to exploit. It takes surprisingly little contact and effort for a target of an influence operation to become an ally. A longtime friendship with a lobbyist, for example, can make one predisposed to trust and feel sympathy for his client's point of view.

Once the diplomatic war with Saudi Arabia intensified in the summer of 2017, Qatar recognized the need for more air cover in Washington. And what better smokescreen than getting Jewish lobbyists to persuade influential—and better yet, staunchly conservative—Jewish community leaders to mysteriously soften their stance on a prominent state funder of anti-Israel terrorist groups?

This effort culminated in a successful influence operation carried out with Qatari money by American lobbyists and agents, specifically Stonington Strategies, run by former kosher steakhouse owner Joey Allaham and the former deputy chief of staff for Sen. Ted Cruz, Nick Muzin.[164]

Muzin grew up in the Toronto Jewish community. He was a good student and a high achiever, completing medical school in the Bronx before switching gears and turning to law school at Yale. Following a marriage to Andrea Michelle Zucker, the daughter of Charleston billionaires Anita and Jerry Zucker, he soon became involved in South Carolina politics, where he helped then-Charleston City Councilmember Tim Scott get elected in Washington, first to the House of Representatives and then to the Senate. He worked as deputy chief-of-staff to Cruz during his 2016 presidential campaign, appearing often with the candidate at Jewish community events.

Allaham couldn't have been more different. He was born into a family of Syrian Jews in Damascus and arrived in America in the early 1990s. He opened several of New York's premiere kosher restaurants, including Prime Grill. One by one, though, Allaham's seemingly successful restaurants began shutting their doors. Towards the end of 2017—when Stonington's contract with the Qataris was in full swing—the Forward reported on the closing of the last of Allaham's restaurants, Prime at the Bently,[165] as he was embroiled in lawsuits over a series of Kosher Passover excursions that he cancelled, never returning his customers' deposits.[166]

Allaham and Muzin saw an opportunity with Trump's election and got to work selling their influence in the Jewish community. In addition to his contacts in the Republican Party and the conservative movement in Washington, Muzin had married into a wealthy and well-connected family. In Manhattan, Allaham's restaurants were upscale; his customers included not just the most important and powerful members of New York Jewish society but, significantly, anyone who'd want access to them, as well. When they partnered to form their lobbying firm, Stonington Strategies, the pair knew they could sell these connections and get rich doing it.

Muzin and Allaham were not Qatar's only lobbyists in the United States. But, by using their credibility to target and compromise some very influential voices, they unquestionably did the most damage to the Jewish community and Israel's supporters in America. Together, the pair received around $7 million in cash from Doha, according to an expose in Tablet.[167] Not only is that an awfully big paycheck for two newly minted lobbyists, but it allowed them to generously spread a lot of dollars around.

Of course, $7 million is just a small fraction of the sums Qatar admits to spending on lobbying activities annually. Most of the money goes to buy the usual PR firms and advertising campaigns, media operators, and former congressmen, generals and ex-staffers who are paid largely to open key office doors to influential people inside the Beltway. It's this last group that's most interesting and, in the case of Stonington Strategies, deeply cynical.

Over the course of a year or more, armed with cash from Doha, Muzin and Allaham launched an influence operation targeting some very prominent leaders in the Jewish and non-Jewish conservative community. They used that money to wine and dine Israel supporters, bring them to Doha, donate to their non-profits and, finally, convince them that Qatar—the patron of Hamas and the Muslim Brotherhood, the ally of Iran—is friendly towards Israel. And, for a time, it seemed like they were succeeding.

The relationships Muzin and Allaham could leverage for Qatar's benefit were tremendously valuable. They enabled them to enlist others with unimpeachable pro-Israel credentials who could, in turn, serve as surrogates for Qatar's interests. When Qatar pays off people with pro-Israel bona fides, it has a downstream effect; others, who might know less about the issues or the region itself will naturally follow the thought-leader.

In a podcast with Jamie Weinstein some months after Muzin and Allaham's pro-Qatar charm offensive, TurningPoint USA's Charlie Kirk, a conservative who is staunchly supportive of Israel, attributed his new but firmly-held pro-Qatar positions to things he'd heard from two of the people Muzin had arranged to financially benefit from the Emirate, Alan Dershowitz and Mort Klein. "Ask Mort Klein about that," Kirk said, pushing back on Weinstein's assertion that Qatar funded Hamas. "I learned from Mort…and ask Alan Dershowitz."[168]

Mort Klein of the Zionist Organization of America (ZOA) has long been known as an uncompromising (if controversial) voice on Israel.[169] "During the first year of the Trump administration," the Forward noted, "Klein's ZOA emerged as the Jewish organization with the most access to some of the president's senior advisors, including Steve Bannon and U.S. Ambassador to Israel David Friedman."[170]

In a 2014 press release, the ZOA had urged the U.S. State Department to designate Qatar as a state sponsor of terrorism, and had accused the emirate of "sponsoring, funding and promoting Nazi-like organizations that want to kill every Jew."[171] By 2018, though, Klein had made a convenient about-face on Qatari support for terrorism and Hamas. ZOA published a long essay on ZOA's website whitewashing Qatar's backing of Israel's enemies. Certainly, if Qatar was kosher enough for Klein, how can you blame others for taking the same position? And it played out in just the way both Muzin and his Qataris paymasters had hoped.

Upon returning from a Muzin- and Allaham-arranged trip to Qatar late in 2017, lawyer and Trump confidant Alan Dershowitz wrote an opinion piece for The Hill that would make readers of his very fine book, The Case for Israel, cringe.[172] "Qatar is quickly becoming the Israel of the Gulf States," he wrote. The Muslim Brotherhood patron, in Dershowitz's telling, was being "surrounded by enemies, subject to boycotts and unrealistic demands, and struggling for its survival." At least the attorney had the sense to dispense with any pretense of independent analysis up-front, with a kind of disclaimer — albeit an embarrassing one: "I just returned from a private visit to Qatar," Dershowitz declared, "at the invitation of and paid for by the Emir."

Soon, the media was asking questions. Was Dershowitz, a longtime friend and neighbor of the president's in Palm Beach, valuable to Qatar as both as a prominent pro-Israel voice and also as a way to influence Donald Trump? Certainly, this must've played into their calculations. "If I had known their purpose with me was maybe to impact the president, I would not have gone," Dershowitz later told the Wall Street Journal.[173] If Dershowitz returned the honorarium he received in Doha, he hasn't spoken of it.

Mike Huckabee, the former Arkansas governor and Fox News host—and, very significantly, father of the president's press secretary—also travelled to Doha on one of Muzin's junkets. Accompanied on the trip by Dershowitz and Klein, Huckabee earned a generous honorarium. In January, Huckabee tweeted about the "surprisingly beautiful, modern, and hospitable" capitol of Doha. Aside from the single supportive tweet, Huckabee hasn't addressed the Gulf dispute publicly, or distanced himself from Qatar, even after Stonington subsequently cut its ties with the emirate. As Mother Jones noted, "So this is how it worked, according to Allaham's disclosure report: Huckabee was paid to visit Qatar, and for its $50,000, the Qatari government got a positive tweet out of him."

It's one thing to bankroll cultural events and hire well-connected former policymakers to run lucrative trade associations, but the chutzpah of trying to convince American Jewish community to brush off Qatar's support for the terrorist enemy Israel faces would take a lot of money and determination.[174]

Thankfully, Muzin and Allaham's aggressive, well-paid jaunt as lobbyists for Qatar soon darkened their reputations in both the tight-knit pro-Israel and conservative communities in Washington, New York and Los Angeles. Their willingness to target longtime opponents of the Muslim Brotherhood, like former RNC Finance Chairman and pro-Israel philanthropist Elliott Broidy, also grated on many in the pro-Israel world. Muzin and Allaham both publicly distanced themselves from Doha in June of 2018. "Stonington Strategies is no longer representing the State of Qatar," Muzin tweeted.[175]

Ultimately, their plan to have the American Jewish community embrace Qatar didn't really work, at least not as well as their Qatari patrons had hoped; however much you spend, you'll have a hard time convincing most people that one of their most potent enemies is really their ally.[176] Israel's political and security establishments already understand this, as evidenced by the multiple Israeli officials who unequivocally assailed Qatar in their recent conversations with me on the sidelines of the 2018 AIPAC conference.

What was most shocking for these Israeli officials is not Qatar's influence campaign itself—after all, this is the country that funds Hamas and promotes the virulently anti-Semitic Muslim Brotherhood—but the Jewish leaders who lent their de facto kosher certification to the emirate. (In one instance, it happened quite literally: one of the Jewish leaders to visit Qatar was Rabbi Menachem Genack, CEO of the Orthodox Union's Kosher Division.)[177]

"The Jewish leaders who became pawns of the Islamist-supporting regime in Qatar and accepted these state-funded trips to Doha did nothing short of betray Israel and the Jewish people," an Israeli diplomat told me. "There has been concern about this campaign at the highest levels in Jerusalem. Those who participated in this disgrace should be held accountable."

THE OPERATION'S POLITICAL GOALS

By design, information operations enlist a diverse cast of players, from reliable, "echo chamber" commentators and media figures to politicians, who would then be moved to act based on the new attitude and information the campaign had inserted into the discussion. This operational aspect is of primary importance; as information operations always work to advance policy interests, in order to succeed, these perceptions must affect policymakers and cause them to alter policy.

Influencers—paid or otherwise—work best when there's a conveyor belt of product for them to comment on, usually a stream of news articles. And one of the biggest stories of the past several years was the

2018 murder of Jamal Khashoggi.[178] Not only did it receive an incredible amount of coverage, but it was used very deliberately as a spark that would ignite policy debates that would advance Qatar's regional agenda. Even now, Khashoggi's murder is waved, like a bloody shirt, to justify downgrading the US-Saudi alliance at a key moment of fragile peace between Israel and its Arab neighbors.[179]

The American public's support for the Jewish State made it difficult for Obama partisans to wage total information war against it, even as they did just that during the intense time of the Iran Deal debate in 2015.[180] The monarchy of Saudi Arabia, by contrast, was vulnerable; it quickly found itself the Designated Villain of a relentless and hostile American press corps.

By the end of the first week of October 2018, when the disappearance of *Washington Post* columnist Jamal Khashoggi set off a global media firestorm, these voices, including many that were prominent in American media, were primed to take advantage—and revenge. [181]Faced with a common enemy, members of the media and policy community who comprised the "echo chamber" that spun and amplified the positions of the Obama administration soon found themselves aligned with a sophisticated Turkish and Qatari information operation to target the US-Saudi alliance.

The narrative focusing on the death of Jamal Khashoggi was to be put into the service of both Qatar and Turkey's main interest, undermining the stability of its rival, Saudi Arabia. When complete, the successful information operation would depict Khashoggi a heroic martyr to independent journalism and freedom, while Saudi Arabia would be the embodiment of evil and callousness. It is clear now that, not only was Khashoggi transmogrified in death into a major front in Qatar's war on its Gulf neighbors; in life, he was Qatar's asset in that war, as well.

The effort to transform Khashoggi from the political operative he was into a journalist and martyr for freedom was an information operation waged largely in the United States. As a columnist for the most widely read and important newspaper in the most important city in the world, Jamal Khashoggi had access to an extremely valuable audience: the policymakers and "smart set" think tankers and government officials who read the *Washington Post* daily. Getting in front of that audience is an opportunity to influence that's worth millions.

But, despite the posthumous lionization of Khashoggi in the press, his English was so poor that he required more than just the several editors he leaned on for help writing his columns. We've subsequently learned that Khashoggi had what could be described as a "handler," crafting the message of his *Washington Post* pieces. This staffer at the Qatar Foundation told the *Post* how she "shaped" the articles he was writing for a US audience.[182]

As the news of Khashoggi's disappearance and death broke, nearly the entire media was abuzz with praise for the late columnist and engaged in an effort to turn him into a martyr for democratic values, free expression and freedom. As the *Post* described him, "[Khashoggi was] a writer of modest influence beyond the Middle East when he was alive. In death, he has become a symbol of a broader struggle for human rights."[183] No outlet did more in the service of cementing that symbolism than the *Washington Post* and its news and editorial staff. Since October, that outlet has functioned unofficially as the most relentless and influential anti-Saudi lobbying shop in the nation's capital. Indeed, the successful campaign of hagiography following his death prompted *Time Magazine* to name Khashoggi and other members of the media "Person of the Year."[184]

Of course, in order to do this, the media largely ignored salient facts about him that emerged almost immediately: his long history as an apologist and propagandist for the Muslim Brotherhood; his youthful collaboration with Osama Bin Laden and al Qaeda in Afghanistan; his antipathy toward both Israel and Shia Muslims; as well as rumors about his questionable and financial links to Qatari intelligence.

Now, shockingly, the *Washington Post* itself largely revealed those rumors to be true.[185] We now know that Jamal Khashoggi was never a journalist—at least, not in the usual sense of the word; he was a highly-partisan operative who worked with a handler to publish propaganda at the behest of the Emirate of Qatar. He was, in other words, an agent of influence.

Rumors have floated inside the Beltway about the contents of Khashoggi's text messages and, potentially, evidence of wire transfers from Qatar found at his residences in Ankara and in Falls Church, Virginia. *The Post's* pre-Christmas release of this information is almost certainly in an effort to get ahead of a story that another outlet is pursuing, and frame some rather explosive revelations in the least damaging way.

In an extensive background portrait of Khashoggi buoyed with accounts from sympathetic friends, reporters Souad Mekhennet and Greg Miller admit that, "text messages between Khashoggi and an executive at Qatar Foundation International show that the executive, Maggie Mitchell Salem, at times shaped the columns he submitted to *The Washington Post*, proposing topics, drafting material and prodding him to take a harder line against the Saudi government." The article also glides past crucial context about the relationships Khashoggi cultivated with Islamists and Muslim Brotherhood figures, especially in recent years, and why these connections are important to the work he was doing on behalf of Qatar.

Still, this report was crucial because the campaign to lionize Khashoggi and to destroy the US-Saudi relationship was built on the fiction that the Saudis had killed a mere journalist. Knowing the truth about Khashoggi—not only his anti-Americanism and pro-Islamism (which, for most of the media, is no sin), but his ties to Qatari information operators—would complicate the narrative greatly. The gory murder of a spy in the process of a rendition to his home country isn't pretty, but it's a far cry from the image the media wanted to present.

In time, though, some journalists and media figures began to question the defensibility of their position and to withdraw to positions that they found more secure. Over the course of the next hours and days, the Security Studies Group (SSG) generated several research products, including backgrounders, articles[186] and interviews that punctured the narrative by linking Khashoggi to the Muslim Brotherhood and other extremist Islamist groups.[187]

At SSG, we had opened the narrative space in the debate for questioning and thoughtfully assessing Khashoggi's Islamist background and sympathies. Foreign policy analyst Matt Brodsky published the first widely-distributed article about the late columnist's Brotherhood connections, "Why is the Media Ignoring the Most Glaring Questions about Jamal Khashoggi?" at the *Spectator*.[188] Soon, others felt emboldened enough to publish aggressive pushbacks on the unwarranted praise for Khashoggi in the mainstream media.

The inevitable hysterical overreaction from the press made it possible for SSG to increase not only the visibility of our message, but the credibility that comes from the public's recognition of blatant media bias. The rancor of the "echo chamber" was best captured by *Post*, which noticed the campaign and tried to do damage control on October 19 with, "Conservatives mount a whisper campaign smearing Khashoggi in defense of Trump":

> In recent days, a cadre of conservative House Republicans allied with Trump has been privately exchanging articles from right-wing outlets that fuel suspicion of Khashoggi, highlighting his association with the Muslim Brotherhood in his youth and raising conspiratorial questions

about his work decades ago as an embedded reporter covering Osama bin Laden.[189]

Our offensive to highlight Khashoggi's Muslim Brotherhood links and pro-Islamist sympathies was so successful that the Qatar-funded Brookings Institute issued a paper on October 19, "On Jamal Khashoggi, the Muslim Brotherhood, and Saudi Arabia," to address (and begrudgingly acknowledge) the columnist's Ikhwan membership and subsequent support for the Islamist movement.[190] Even devoid of context for most readers, *The Post's* recent acknowledgement of these connections—to the Brotherhood, as well as to elements of the Qatari network of foundations in Doha and Washington, especially—offers a great deal of vindication for our efforts in the service of accurate analysis.

This didn't stop many commentators and media voices in the United States from partaking in this influence operation for reasons of their own. But before the partisan American "echo chamber" could engage, though, foreign sources would shape the stream of facts that could be molded into a potent narrative. As Brad Patty and Nick Short concluded in their assessment of this information campaign, SSG's "Firehoses in the Khashoggi Case," this happened within hours of Khashoggi's disappearance in Ankara.[191] Turkey took advantage of the silence from Saudi Arabia in the crucial first 36 hours of the controversy to shift the narrative from Khashoggi's disappearance to leaks of increasingly brutal and graphic reports of his death at the Saudi Consulate in Istanbul. Officials from Turkey's Erdogan government—a longtime regional rival of the Kingdom's power and influence and, lately, an Islamist nation building a growing alliance with Qatar and Iran—began to distribute weaponized, unverified information to the press. They gave it directly to reporters at prominent American media outlets, especially David Kirkpatrick at the *New York Times* and a massive team from Khashoggi's alma mater the *Washington Post*.

Another major source of news about Khashoggi was, unsurprisingly, Qatar's al Jazeera, as well as Middle East Eye, a relatively new outlet with ties of its own to Qatar. Some of the most scandalous, unverified stories in the press were sourced to Turkish officials and conformed "by a high-ranking Arab official."[192] There is a very high likelihood that that high-ranking official was from Qatar. For months, US major media outlets and high-profile "echo chamber" pundits were knowingly assuming the risk of broadcasting false Turkish and Qatari narratives, without adequately informing their readers of the risk being passed on to them.

By December 2018—when the campaign had done great harm to the US-Saudi relationship and America's alliances in the Middle East—Erdogan was publicly bragging about his part in this successful information operation, and as well he should.[193] It caused tremendous damage to the Kingdom and the Crown Prince, but also elevated Turkey and Qatar and gave it leverage to use with the US and others.

Once President Trump released a robust statement supporting the US-Saudi alliance, intense political pressure was felt from anti-Trump forces in the American media, which pushed Democrats toward Qatar and Iran, and away from Saudi Arabia.

Suddenly, the alliance had become a partisan issue; prominent Democrats in Congress began calling for a reevaluation of American policy toward the country. The intensity with which the Kingdom's critics have attacked the US-Saudi relationship specifically points to more than just a target of opportunity. These critics could be placed into (at least) one of the following categories: (a) a pro-Iran position; (b) a pro-Islamist/Muslim Brotherhood position; and (c) anti-Trump. Often—as with the case of the *Washington Post*—it is a combination of all three.

Led by Sen. Chris Murphy and Elizabeth Warren, voices from the political Left seemed to outdo each other in berating Crown Prince

Mohammed bin Salman, with whom President Trump and members of his administration have warm relations. They are trying to use outrage over Khashoggi's death to force a Saudi surrender in the war in Yemen; and end to arms sales, a break in US-Saudi relations, or even to depose Saudi Crown Prince Muhammad bin Salman from his position in the Kingdom's order of succession. This, of course, was the Qatari policy aim at the conclusion of the successful information operation all along.

EPILOGUE

Over the last half-decade, many Americans have gotten a peek into the dark world of information operators-for-hire, where political activism combines with media skullduggery. The more blatant and ham-fisted the operation, the more the contours of these kinds of operations become familiar, even to those who're only occasional consumers of news.

Once you see how information and political warfare works, it's nearly impossible to un-see. And, like the familiar process of being "red-pilled," the first instinct is to find a new tribe (usually online) with whom the "secret knowledge" can be discussed, once the scales have fallen from one's eyes. Those newly-cynical observers of the scene—many new to politics—will, unfortunately, be tempted to dive deep into any number of conspiracy theories that are not supported by facts or sober analysis. This might be unfortunate, but it is unavoidable.

It's tempting to see operators' machinations and a deliberate, well-executed plan behind everything. That's only partially true, however. Yes, professionals are paid to try and manipulate public discourse in ways that benefit their clients or ideological allies; there are an awful lot of them these days, and they don't stop working and spinning. They work every major political news story or controversy—but they're even more identifiable on the more minor stories. It takes effort to move a story from the fringes to the mainstream, and that's exactly what information operators get paid for. But they're not all-powerful or infallible, and they make plenty of mistakes. Sometimes a narrative just won't catch fire, regardless of the assets a campaign might bring to it.

Rather than be overwhelmed and feel powerless against dark forces, Americans taking their first hard look at the way political warfare works need to feel like they can be a part of the process and agitate for their interests. Their tweets, blog posts, emails, and text messages are all raw material for political warfare campaigns.

Nevertheless, these operations often work—at least on some element of the population. And, needless to say, for millions of Americans to believe things which are not true is immensely damaging to the fabric that binds together the American polity. When these untrue things pit Americans against one another, it's a far more serious situation for the future or the health of the republic. Sincere accusations of treason in modern democratic life are serious things; in another time, they'd be similar to accusations of heresy.

POLICY SUGGESTIONS

The scope of policy changes the United States government needs to undertake to deal with the issues discussed in this book are, admittedly, massive in scope. In a time of deep civilizational crisis, most of our foreign problems are the inevitable consequences of our domestic strife.

First, the constellation of officials in government in the national security and intelligence universe must begin with the recognition that Islamist movements operate to the detriment of American foreign and domestic policy. These groups are ideological and, as such, run at cross-purposes to the interests of both America's physical security and its constitutional regime, such as it is. In foreign policy, US government must not promote Islamist movements like the Muslim Brotherhood and assist in its quest of toppling the regimes and governments of our allies in the Middle East. Further, it should support the efforts of these allies in rooting-out and isolating such malefactors. Domestically, the US government should return to vigilance when it comes to investigating and prosecuting material support for both foreign and home-grown Islamist terror activity.

Next, the US must re-evaluate both its foreign and economic policy with regards to Qatar, beginning with the recognition that Doha's interests conflict with those of the United States and its allies in the region. As more Gulf States head towards normalization with Israel, Qatar's state-sponsored propaganda—much of it both anti-Semitic and meant to destabilize its neighbors as they take steps toward a US-encouraged peace—illustrates the sharp and yawning contrast between US allies and adversaries in the region. In a geopolitical sense, Qatar's alliance with Turkey and Iran undermines not only American efforts in the Middle East, but in Europe and NATO as well.

As we have seen, the US military presence at the al Udid Air Base in Qatar acts as a massive Qatari influence operation on our armed forces as well as our diplomatic and military decision-making processes. Both Qatar and Turkey are increasingly Islamist countries which house military assets—for this reason, both are long- and medium-term strategic liabilities. Like Turkey's Incirlik Air Base, the presence of our armed forces do more to hamper American flexibility in foreign policy than to project American power. This is even more true of diplomatic conflicts than military ones. Recognizing that the United States needs operating bases in the Middle East, the US military should look to other, more stable allied countries, like the United Arab Emirates, to host military installations.

The larger issue of foreign influence and information operations, however, is a more complicated one. As discussed, both allied and adversarial nations have the right to present their case to the American people in the form of paid lobbyists or advocates. This isn't necessarily nefarious in all cases. If being paid, these lobbyists are currently required to register as foreign agents, including oftentimes onerous disclosures with contacts in media and government. These kinds of disclosures shed much needed light on the sources of messages injected into the public debate.

In a healthy and functional state, a nation's educational system is geared towards creating and nurturing the beliefs and habits of that regime's idea of the virtuous man. Tragically, modern America is neither healthy nor functional, and its educational system is geared not toward perpetuating the regime, but toward building a revolution against an unjust state. The institutional Left doesn't need foreign cash in order to justify its messaging against America as founded, but it certainly doesn't help. Foreign investment in American educational institutions—and it is an investment, rather than mere philanthropy—must be stopped at every level. This will require legislation, and it will be contentious with the universities and municipalities benefitting from Qatari, Chinese and other states' largesse, but it is necessary in order to maintain even the smallest amount of integrity in our education system.

More low-hanging fruit: Congress must impose harsh penalties for media outlets operating in the United States that are foreign- or state-owned and/or run, yet refuse to disclose this to the FCC, as now required by law.

Information operations originating from American voices are another matter. Our open society and the free flow of information makes the criminalization of political messages legally impossible and leaves the American citizen potentially vulnerable to foreign information operations and campaigns meant to shape public policy or elections. The Democrats' and media's enthusiasm for the Russia Hoax showed the extent to which partisan enmity can wipe away considerations of free expression and considered debate. The country has entered a revolutionary period, where ideological considerations easily override the principles on which the nation was once founded. If, as some on the Left insist, speech designated as 'hateful' can be circumscribed on national security grounds, there's no reason to believe speech which can be alleged to dovetail with foreign messaging can't be similarly circumscribed. It is entirely possible (or even probable) to find that, within the next half-decade, such speech is criminalized. What happens next to America is beyond the scope of this book.

NOTES

[1] Abu Amer, Adnan. "Qatar pledges to keep money pipeline open to Gaza Strip." Al Monitor. https://www.al-monitor.com/pulse/originals/2019/02/palestine-israel-gaza-hamas-qatar-grant-billion-amount-aid.html#ixzz6NbbngWGk

[2] "How Qatar Targets America's Allies in the New Middle East." Security Studies Group. https://securitystudies.org/how-qatar-targets-americas-allies-in-the-new-middle-east/

[3] Patty, Brad. "The Role of Fomenting Revolutions in Qatari Grand Strategy." Security Studies Group. https://securitystudies.org/the-role-of-fomenting-revolutions-in-qatari-grand-strategy/

[4] Reaboi, David. "Why The Media Is At War With Saudi Arabia." The Federalist. https://thefederalist.com/2019/04/10/media-war-saudi-arabia/

[5] Patty, Brad. "Qatar's Role in the Current Middle East Crisis." Security Studies Group. https://securitystudies.org/qatars-role-current-middle-east-crisis/

[6] "American Muslims for Palestine." NGO Monitor. March 23, 2020. https://www.ngo-monitor.org/ngos/american-muslims-for-palestine-amp/

[7] Oprea, Meg. "Americans Will Accept Islam Once the Left Stops Giving It Special Privileges." The Federalist. https://thefederalist.com/2016/11/17/americans-will-accept-islam-once-the-left-stops-giving-it-special-privileges/

[8] Horowitz, David. Unholy Alliance: Radical Islam And the American Left. Regnery Publishing. (2006)

[9] McCarthy, Andrew C. The Grand Jihad: How Islam and the Left Sabotage America. Regnery Publishing (2010)

[10] "Shaykh Ubayd al-Jaabiree on Sayyid Qutb." SalafiTalk.net website. http://www.salafitalk.net/st/viewmessages.cfm?Forum=32&Topic=11627

[11] Cilizza, Chris. "Just 7 percent of journalists are Republicans. That's far fewer than even a decade ago." Washington Post. https://www.washingtonpost.com/news/the-fix/wp/2014/05/06/just-7-percent-of-journalists-are-republicans-thats-far-less-than-even-a-decade-ago/

[12] Shafer, Jack and Tucker Doherty. "The Media Bubble Is Worse Than You Think." Politico. https://www.politico.com/magazine/story/2017/04/25/media-bubble-real-journalism-jobs-east-coast-215048

[13] Noyes, Rich. "Study: Economic Boom Largely Ignored as TV's Trump Coverage Hits 92% Negative." Newsbusters. https://www.newsbusters.org/blogs/nb/rich-noyes/2018/10/09/study-econ-boom-ignored-tv-trump-coverage-hits-92-percent-negative

[14] Reaboi, David. "Post-Midterms: The Democratic Party's Radicalized Foreign Policy." The American Mind. https://americanmind.org/post/post-midterms-the-democratic-partys-radicalized-foreign-policy/

[15] Taylor, SJ. "Stalin's Apologist: Walter Duranty: The New York Times's Man in Moscow." Oxford University Press (1990).

[16] Kornbluh, Peter. "'My Dearest Fidel': An ABC Journalist's Secret Liaison With Fidel Castro." Politico. https://www.politico.com/magazine/story/2018/04/20/cuba-fidel-castro-affair-lisa-howard-218007

[17] Christian, Shirley. "Pro-Sandinista Journalists Link US Press to CIA." Miami Herald https://www.cia.gov/library/readingroom/docs/CIA-RDP90-00845R000100610001-9.pdf (May 4, 1981)

[18] Committee For Accuracy In Middle East Reporting And Analysis. CAMERA website. https://www.camera.org/article/topic/media-corrections

[19] "Who We Are." ALBA, the Abraham Lincoln Brigade Archives website. https://alba-valb.org/who-we-are/

20 "Henri Cartier-Bresson With the Abraham Lincoln Brigade in Spain." Smithsonian Magazine. https://www.smithsonianmag.com/videos/category/history/henri-cartier-bressons-with-the-abraham-lin/

21 McCain, John. "Salute to a Communist." New York Times. https://www.nytimes.com/2016/03/25/opinion/john-mccain-salute-to-a-communist.html

22 Saad, Linda. "Americans, but Not Liberal Democrats, Mostly Pro-Israel." Gallup. https://news.gallup.com/poll/247376/americans-not-liberal-democrats-mostly-pro-israel.aspx

23 Reaboi, David and Kyle Shideler. "Combatting Political Islam." Claremont Review of Books. https://claremontreviewofbooks.com/digital/combating-political-islam (2016)

24 Reaboi, David. "Ben Rhodes Reveals How Obama Duped America Into The Dangerous Iran Deal." https://thefederalist.com/2016/05/09/ben-rhodes-reveals-how-obama-duped-america-into-the-dangerous-iran-deal/ The Federalist. (2016)

25 Shariah: The Threat to America. Center for Security Policy Press. https://www.centerforsecuritypolicy.org/2010/09/13/shariah-the-threat-to-america/ (2010)

26 Levin, Bess. "Jared Kushner Had A Very Intimate Reunion With His Favorite Saudi Prince." https://www.vanityfair.com/news/2019/03/jared-kushner-saudi-arabia-mbs-meeting Vanity Fair (2019)

27 "Mohammed bin Salman described Khashoggi as 'dangerous Islamist.'" Al Jazeera. https://www.aljazeera.com/news/2018/11/mohammed-bin-salman-khashoggi-dangerous-islamist-181102100634537.html (2018)

28 "Bin Salman: Muslim Brotherhood 'incubator for terrorists.'" Egypt Today. https://www.egypttoday.com/Article/1/46574/Bin-Salman-Muslim-Brotherhood-incubator-for-terrorists (2018)

[29] Reaboi, David. "Why Should We Care About Qatar's Influence?" Security Studies Group. https://securitystudies.org/why-should-we-care-about-qatars-influence (2019)

[30] "What are the 13 demands given to Qatar?" Associated Press. https://gulfnews.com/world/gulf/qatar/what-are-the-13-demands-given-to-qatar-1.2048118 (2017)

[31] "Strong Words in Private from MbZ at Idex—Bashes Iran, Qatar, Russia." WikiLeaks. https://wikileaks.org/plusd/cables/09ABUDHABI193_a.html (February, 25, 2009)

[32] Emerson, Steven. "The Inside Story of How John Kerry Secretly Lobbied to Get CAIR Removed From UAE's Terrorist Organization List." IPT News. https://www.investigativeproject.org/5758/the-inside-story-of-how-john-kerry-secretly (2017)

[33] David Reaboi and Kyle Shideler. "Combatting Political Islam." Claremont Institute. https://claremontreviewofbooks.com/digital/combating-political-islam/ (2016)

[34] 4th Annual Valley Banquet. CAIR California. https://ca.cair.com/losangeles/event/4th-annual-valley-banquet/

[35] Brodey, Sam. "Who's afraid of Ilhan Omar? Saudi Arabia, for one." MinnPost. https://www.minnpost.com/national/2018/12/whos-afraid-of-ilhan-omar-saudi-arabia-for-one (2018)

[36] "Khashoggi Case- Analysis of an Information Operation." Security Studies Group. https://securitystudies.org/khashoggi-case-analysis-of-an-information-operation (2018)

[37] Fisher, Alan. "Major business leaders boycott Saudi summit over Khashoggi case." https://www.aljazeera.com/news/2018/10/major-business-leaders-boycott-saudi-summit-khashoggi-case-181013121304654.html

[38] "Business is boycotting Saudi Arabia's big conference. Here's who's still going." CNN News. https://www.abcactionnews.com/news/national/business-is-boycotting-saudi-arabias-big-conference-heres-whos-still-going

[39] Ryan, Reed and Simon Vozick-Levinson. "Mariah Carey to Perform in Saudi Arabia Despite Calls for Boycott." Rolling Stone. https://www.rollingstone.com/music/music-news/mariah-carey-saudi-arabia-boycott-787538/

[40] "CODEPINK announces launch of Boycott Saudi Arabia Campaign." https://www.codepink.org/codepink_announces_launch_of_boycott_saudi_arabia_campaign CodePink.

[41] Markay, Lachlan. "Lobbying Shop Inks New Saudi Contract Amid Khashoggi Backlash." The Daily Beast. https://www.thedailybeast.com/lobbying-shop-inks-new-saudi-contract-amid-khashoggi-backlash

[42] "Why Yousef Al Qaradawi is on Saudi Arabia and UAE's Qatar-linked terrorism list – video." The National. https://www.thenational.ae/world/why-yousef-al-qaradawi-is-on-saudi-arabia-and-uae-s-qatar-linked-terrorism-list-video-1.41115

[43] Shideler, Kyle. "Why The United States Should Officially Label This Muslim Brotherhood Leader A Terrorist." The Federalist. https://thefederalist.com/2019/01/29/united-states-officially-label-muslim-brotherhood-leader-terrorist/

[44] McElroy, Damian. "US advisers quit Qatar role as emir dines with Muslim Brotherhood leader." The National. https://www.thenational.ae/world/gcc/us-advisers-quit-qatar-role-as-emir-dines-with-muslim-brotherhood-leader-1.737981

[45] "President Trump's Approach To Saudi Arabia." NPR Weekend Edition Sunday. https://www.npr.org/2018/11/25/670631143/president-trumps-approach-to-saudi-arabia

[46] Foarde, Connor. "Congress weighs terror label for Muslim Brotherhood." Washington Times. https://www.washingtontimes.com/news/2018/jul/11/congress-weighs-terror-label-for-muslim-brotherhoo/

[47] "About Qatar." Qatar Ministry of Municipality and Environment. http://www.mme.gov.qa/cui/view.dox?id=954&contentID=1409&siteID=2

[48] "GDP Per Capita." World Bank https://data.worldbank.org/indicator/NY.GDP.PCAP.CD?year_high_desc=true

[49] "Qatar Airways Completes Move To New Doha Airport." Associated Press. https://web.archive.org/web/20140527193613/http:/bigstory.ap.org/article/qatar-airways-completes-move-new-doha-airport (2014)

[50] "Population Total: Qatar." The WorldBank. https://data.worldbank.org/indicator/SP.POP.TOTL?locations=QA

[51] Wisher, Dane. "The Moral Conflict of Living and Working in Qatar." The Billfold. https://www.thebillfold.com/2015/06/the-moral-conflict-of-living-and-working-in-qatar/

[52] Ghani, Faras. "Qatar moves to announce abolishment of kafala system." Al Jazeera. https://www.aljazeera.com/news/2019/10/qatar-moves-announce-abolishment-kafala-system-191017070750729.html

[53] "Migrant Workers Rights with Four Years to the Qatar 2022 World Cup: Reality Check." Amnesty International. https://www.amnesty.org/en/latest/campaigns/2019/02/reality-check-migrant-workers-rights-with-four-years-to-qatar-2022-world-cup/

[54] "Tourist Information: Qatar Population and Expat Nationalities." Online Qatar. https://www.onlineqatar.com/visiting/tourist-information/qatar-population-and-expat-nationalities

[55] "Qatar Population Growth Rate 1950-2020." MacroTrends.net. https://www.macrotrends.net/countries/QAT/qatar/population-growth-rate

[56] Pattisson, Pete and Roshan Sedhai. "Qatar's migrant workers beg for food as Covid-19 infections rise." The Guardian. https://www.theguardian.com/global-

development/2020/may/07/qatars-migrant-workers-beg-for-food-as-covid-19-infections-rise

[57] Gaddis, John Lewis. The Cold War: A New History. Penguin Press. (2005)

[58] "The Al Thani." Persian Gulf States: A Country Study. Library of Congress. http://countrystudies.us/persian-gulf-states/79.htm

[59] Olidort, Jacob. "Who Was Ibn 'Abd al-Wahhab?" Washington Institute. https://www.washingtoninstitute.org/policy-analysis/view/who-was-ibn-abd-al-wahhab

[60] Mouline, Nabil. "Clerics of Islam: Religious Authority and Political Power in Saudi Arabia." Yale Scholarship Online. https://yale.universitypressscholarship.com/view/10.12987/yale/9780300178906.001.0001/upso-9780300178906-chapter-3

[61] Holla, Anand. "Looking back to how oil exploration started in Qatar." Gulf Times. https://m.gulf-times.com/story/526227/Looking-back-to-how-oil-exploration-started-in-Qatar

[62] "The Foundation of the New Terrorism." National Commission on Terrorist Attacks Upon the United States (9/11 Commission Report). https://govinfo.library.unt.edu/911/report/911Report_Ch2.htm

[63] Jones, Benjamin. "9 Bedford Row Report on the History of the Muslim Brotherhood." 9 Bedford Row International. http://9bri.com/9-bedford-row-report-on-the-history-of-the-muslim-brotherhood/ (2015)

[64] "Egypt says 6 Muslim Brotherhood killed in Cairo shootout." Associated Press. https://abcnews.go.com/International/wireStory/egypt-muslim-brotherhood-killed-cairo-shootout-65819010 (2019)

[65] Al-Qaradawi, Yusuf. "Islamic Education and Hassan Al Banna." (1984)

[66] Coughlin, Stephen. "Catastrophic Failure: Blindfolding America in the Face of Jihad." Center for Security Policy Press (2015)

[67] Johnson, Ian. "A Mosque in Munich: Nazis, the CIA, and the Muslim Brotherhood in the West." Houghton Mifflin (2010)

[68] Steinberg, Guido. "Germany and the Muslim Brotherhood." Foreign Policy Research Institute. https://www.fpri.org/docs/chapters/201303.west_and_the_muslim_brotherhood_after_the_arab_spring.chapter5.pdf (2013)

[69] "Muslim Students Association." The Investigative Project On Terrorism Dossier. https://www.investigativeproject.org/documents/misc/31.pdf (Undated)

[70] Al-Hasam Sadeq. "Tarbiya Plan for Islamic Schools." Islamic Society of North America. https://isna.net/wp-content/uploads/2016/10/tarbiya_plan_for_islamic_schools.pdf (Undated)

[71] Siddiqi, Shamim. "Methodology of Dawah Ilallah in American Perspective." Forum for Islamic Work. http://www.dawahinamericas.com/bookspdf/MethodologyofDawah.pdf (1989)

[72] Shideler, Kyle and David Daoud. "International Institute of Islamic Thought (IIIT): The Muslim Brotherhood's Think Tank." Center for Security Policy. https://www.centerforsecuritypolicy.org/wp-content/uploads/2014/07/IIIT-Backgrounder-final-07-28-14-1.pdf (2014)

[73] Qutb, Sayyid. "Social Justice in Islam, Revised Edition." Islamic Publications International. (2000)

[74] Skovgaard-Petersen, Jakob and Bettina Graf, Eds. The Global Mufti: The Phenomenon of Yusuf al-Qaradawi. Columbia University Press. (2009)

[75] Wright, Lawrence. "The Rebellion Within: An Al Qaeda mastermind questions terrorism." The New Yorker. https://www.newyorker.com/magazine/2008/06/02/the-rebellion-within (2008)

[76] "Yusuf al-Qaradawi." Religious Literacy Project, Harvard Divinity School. https://rlp.hds.harvard.edu/faq/yusuf-al-qaradawi

[77] Helfont, Samuel. "Islam and Islamism Today: The Case of Yusuf al-Qaradawi." Foreign Policy Research Institute. https://www.fpri.org/article/2010/01/islam-and-islamism-today-the-case-of-yusuf-al-qaradawi/ (2010)

[78] "Yusuf al-Qaradawi." Religious Literacy Project, Harvard Divinity School. https://rlp.hds.harvard.edu/faq/yusuf-al-qaradawi

[79] Warren, David H. "Qatari Support for the Muslim Brotherhood is More Than Just Realpolitik, it has a Long, Personal History." https://www.academia.edu/34343584/David_H._Warren_Qatari_Support_for_the_Muslim_Brotherhood_is_More_Than_Just_Realpolitik_-_It_Has_a_Long_Personal_History Maydan. (2017)

[80] Tweet from David Weinberg. https://twitter.com/DavidAWeinberg/status/1004005894902964228 June 5, 2018.

[81] Stapley, Karen. Portrait of Sir Lewis Pelly. https://www.qdl.qa/en/portrait-sir-lewis-pelly (2014)

[82] Toth, Anthony, *Qatar: Historical Background, A Country Study*. Library of Congress Federal Research Division. http://countrystudies.us/persian-gulf-states/68.htm (1993)

[83] "US Pulls out of Saudi Arabia." BBC News. http://news.bbc.co.uk/2/hi/middle_east/2984547.stm (2003)

[84] Riedel, Bruce and Bilal Y. Saab. "Al Qaeda's Third Front: Saudi Arabia." Washington Quarterly. https://www.brookings.edu/wp-content/uploads/2016/06/spring_al_qaeda_riedel.pdf (2008)

[85] "Analysis: Qatar as Possible Nerve Center for U.S. Invasion of Iraq." NPR All Things Considered. https://legacy.npr.org/programs/atc/transcripts/2002/oct/021003.seelye.html (2002)

[86] Burkeman, Olivier. "America signals withdrawal of troops from Saudi Arabia." The Guardian. https://www.theguardian.com/world/2003/apr/30/usa.iraq (2003)

[87] "Al Udeid Air Force Base in Doha, Qatar." MilitaryBases.com. https://militarybases.com/overseas/qatar/al-udeid/

[88] Taylor, Adam. "As Trump tries to end 'endless wars,' America's biggest Mideast base is getting bigger." Washington Post. https://www.washingtonpost.com/world/as-trump-tries-to-end-endless-wars-americas-biggest-mideast-base-is-getting-bigger/2019/08/20/47ac5854-bab4-11e9-8e83-4e6687e99814_story.html (2019)

[89] Diaz, Daniella. "Mattis makes unannounced visit to Qatar." CNN. https://www.cnn.com/2017/09/28/politics/secretary-of-defense-mattis-unannounced-visit-qatar/index.html

[90] Lake, Eli and Josh Rogin. "Ambassador Anne Patterson, the Controversial Face of America's Egypt Policy." Daily Beast. https://www.thedailybeast.com/ambassador-anne-patterson-the-controversial-face-of-americas-egypt-policy

[91] Johnson, Eliana. "White House pushing back against Mattis appointment." Politico. https://www.politico.com/story/2017/03/jim-mattis-appointment-white-house-pushback-anne-patterson-235633

[92] "US-Qatar Business Council & US Chamber Host Reception to Honor Amir of Qatar." US-Qatar Business Council. https://www.usqbc.org/news/us-qatar-business-council-us-chamber-host-reception-to-honor-amir-of-qatar (2018)

[93] Levitt, Matthew. "Testimony: Assessing the U.S.-Qatar Relationship." House Foreign Affairs Subcommittee on the Middle East and North Africa. https://docs.house.gov/meetings/FA/FA13/20170726/106329/HHRG-115-FA13-Wstate-LevittM-20170726.pdf (2017)

[94] Al-Ansari, Salman. "How the 9/11 mastermind found safe harbor in Qatar." The Hill. https://thehill.com/blogs/pundits-blog/international/345437-how-the-9-11-mastermind-found-safe-harbor-in-qatar (2017)

[95] Bernays, Edward. Crystalizing Public Opinion. IG Publishing. (1995)

[96] Bernays, Edward. Propaganda. IG Publishing. (1995)

[97] Jones, Bryony and Eliza Mackintosh. "What is Kompromat?" CNN. https://www.cnn.com/2017/01/11/politics/what-is-kompromat/index.html (2018)

[98] Trumpbour, Robert. "End of blue-collar journalism: Should reporting become less professional?" Salon. https://www.salon.com/2017/04/03/should-journalism-become-less-professional_partner (2017)

[99] Assuras, Thalia. "How the GI Bill Changed America." CBS News Sunday Morning. https://www.cbsnews.com/news/how-the-gi-bill-changed-america (2008)

[100] Sheikh, Knvul. "Nice Niche: How to Build and Keep Up with a Beat." Open Notebook. https://www.theopennotebook.com/2019/06/04/nice-niche-how-to-build-and-keep-up-with-a-beat (2019)

[101] Griner, David. "U.S. Newspapers Make $40 Billion Less From Ads Today Than in 2000." Adweek. https://www.adweek.com/digital/us-newspapers-make-40-billion-less-ads-today-2000-160966 (2014)

[102] Smith, Lee. "Spies are the new Journalists." Tablet. https://www.tabletmag.com/sections/news/articles/spies-are-the-new-journalists (2020)

[103] "The 6 Companies That Own (Almost) All Media." WebFX.com. https://www.webfx.com/blog/internet/the-6-companies-that-own-almost-all-media-infographic/

[104] Barber, Kayleigh. "How The New York Times' Taylor Lorenz gets teenagers to talk about their digital habits." Digiday. https://digiday.com/media/dont-really-use-email-new-york-times-taylor-lorenz-works (2020)

[105] Doran, Michael. "Obama's Secret Iran Strategy." Mosaic. https://www.hudson.org/research/10989-obama-s-secret-iran-strategy (2015)

[106] Reaboi, David. "Ben Rhodes Reveals How Obama Duped America Into The Dangerous Iran Deal." The Federalist. https://thefederalist.com/2016/05/09/ben-rhodes-reveals-how-obama-duped-america-into-the-dangerous-iran-deal/ (2016)

[107] Samuels, David. "The Aspiring Novelist Who Became Obama's Foreign-Policy Guru. How Ben Rhodes rewrote the rules of diplomacy for the digital age." https://www.nytimes.com/2016/05/08/magazine/the-aspiring-novelist-who-became-obamas-foreign-policy-guru.html New York Times Magazine (2016)

[108] Smith, Lee. "Wayne Barrett, Donald Trump, and the Death of the American Press." Tablet. https://www.hudson.org/research/13387-wayne-barrett-donald-trump-and-the-death-of-the-american-press (2017)

[109] "Columnist: This is every Muslim's worst nightmare." CNN. https://www.cnn.com/videos/world/2019/03/15/muslims-worst-nightmare-new-zealand-christchurch-mosque-shooting-sot-vpx-ctn.cnn

[110] Mehdi Hasan Facebook. https://www.facebook.com/watch/?v=389739021758969

[111] Velshi, Ali. "Why Trump downplays threat of white nationalism in the U.S." MSNBC. https://www.msnbc.com/ali-velshi/watch/why-trump-downplays-threat-of-white-nationalism-in-the-u-s-1460357699821

[112] Mehdi Hasan biography. Al Jazeera. https://www.aljazeera.com/profile/mehdi-hasan.html

[113] Reaboi, David. "Qatar Shows Two Faces to the World." Jewish Journal. https://jewishjournal.com/cover_story/298975/qatar-shows-two-faces-to-the-world/

[114] Mauro, Ryan. "Questioning Qatar's Terror Financing? Here Are the Facts." Clarion Project. https://clarionproject.org/questioning-qatars-terror-financing-facts/

[115] Tweet from @TamimBinHamad https://twitter.com/TamimBinHamad/status/1140668298889179136

[116] "President Erdogan speaks about Morsi's death." TRT World Youtube. https://www.youtube.com/watch?v=zAO7Q0xjhAQ

[117] "Mohamed Morsi's death: World reaction." Al Jazeera. https://www.aljazeera.com/news/2019/06/mohamed-morsi-death-world-reaction-190617162635604.html

[118] "Qatari FM: We do not support the Muslim Brotherhood." Al Monitor. https://www.al-monitor.com/pulse/fr/politics/2015/02/qatar-foreign-minister-gulf-hezbollah-brotherhood.html#ixzz6NnPqwLr8

[119] Tweet from David Reaboi. https://twitter.com/davereaboi/status/1140727375879180289

[120] "Turkey, Qatar Only Countries to React to Morsi's Death." Egyptian Streets. https://egyptianstreets.com/2019/06/18/turkey-qatar-only-countries-to-react-to-morsis-death/

[121] "English text of Morsi's Constitutional Declaration." Ahram. http://english.ahram.org.eg/News/58947.aspx

[122] Kingsley, Patrick. "Protesters across Egypt call for Mohamed Morsi to go." The Guardian. https://www.theguardian.com/world/2013/jun/30/mohamed-morsi-egypt-protests

[123] "Washington Post Hints What Others Have Known: Jamal Khashoggi Was a Paid Qatari Intelligence Asset." RedState. https://www.redstate.com/streiff/2018/12/26/washington-post-hints-others-known-jamal-khashoggi-paid-qatari-intelligence-asset/

[124] "A terrorism label that would hurt: Washington Post Editorial." Washington Post. https://www.oregonlive.com/opinion/2017/02/a_terrorism_label_that_would_h.html

[125] Poole, Patrick. "Ted Cruz Renews Call to Designate Muslim Brotherhood a Terrorist Group." PJMedia. https://pjmedia.com/homeland-security/patrick-

poole/2018/09/12/ted-cruz-renews-call-to-designate-muslim-brotherhood-a-terrorist-group-n100637

[126] Haddera, Wael. "Egypt's regime must answer for Morsi's death. Other dictatorships are watching." Washington Post. https://cc.bingj.com/cache.aspx?q=Wael+Haddara+washington+post&d=5050052801593371&mkt=en-US&setlang=en-US&w=BMPcFeiFZtn4f6d4c4YgVYXhMdtGvtBs

[127] "The unjust death of Mohamed Morsi shows how far Egypt has regressed." https://www.washingtonpost.com/opinions/global-opinions/the-unjust-death-of-mohamed-morsi-shows-how-far-egypt-has-regressed/2019/06/18/d0db6c96-91ec-11e9-aadb-74e6b2b46f6a_story.html?noredirect=on

[128] "Wael Haddara resigned from the board of the Muslim Association of Canada. The new president is Yasser Mohammed." Point de Bascule. https://pointdebascule-canada.ca/wael-haddara-resigned-from-the-board-of-the-muslim-association-of-canada-the-new-president-is-yasser-mohammed/

[129] Al-Houthi, Mohammed. "Houthi leader: We want peace for Yemen, but Saudi airstrikes must stop." Washington Post. https://www.washingtonpost.com/news/global-opinions/wp/2018/11/09/houthi-leader-we-want-peace-for-yemen-but-saudi-airstrikes-must-stop/?tid=ss_tw&utm_term=.d8e4ee20994c&noredirect=on

[130] Lenarz, Julie. "Who Are the Houthis and Why Do They Shout "Death to America"?" The Tower. https://cc.bingj.com/cache.aspx?q=%E2%80%9CAllah+is+the+Greatest.+Death+to+America.+Death+to+Israel.+Curse+on+the+Jews.+Victory+to+Islam.%E2%80%9D&d=4629227608083967&mkt=en-US&setlang=en-US&w=KmaEVym3PUw5IWhZ_YeOkzttaZBqjFrY

[131] Tweet from Saudi Foreign Ministry. https://twitter.com/KSAmofaEN/status/1140932146149953536 (June 18, 2019)

[132] Karam, Joyce. "Saudi Crown Prince: We will expel Muslim Brotherhood from our schools." The National. https://www.thenational.ae/world/mena/saudi-crown-prince-we-will-expel-muslim-brotherhood-from-our-schools-1.714241 (2018)

133 Davis, Charles. "The Intercept, a billionaire-funded public charity, cuts back." Columbia Journalism Review. https://www.cjr.org/business_of_news/layoffs-the-intercept.php

134 "The Definitive Glenn Greenwald Takedown." American Power. https://americanpowerblog.blogspot.com/2010/07/definitive-glenn-greenwald-takedown.html

135 Greenwald, Glenn. "Meet the Muslim-American Leaders the FBI And NSA Have Been Spying On." The Intercept. https://theintercept.com/2014/07/09/under-surveillance/

136 "Qatar Airways strengthens relationship with CNN International." Arab News. https://www.arabnews.com/corporate-news/news/849016

137 Reaboi, David. "Railing against Islamophobia, and anti-Trump, too." Washington Times. https://www.washingtontimes.com/news/2019/mar/28/railing-against-islamophobia-and-anti-trump-too/

138 Codevilla, Angelo. "For Years, Qatar Has Been Corrupting the National Security Deep State." Security Studies Group. https://securitystudies.org/qatar-is-corrupting-the-national-security-deep-state/

139 Bryson, Jennifer. "Is Rumsfeld's Criticism of Al-Jazeera Justified?" Newsmax. https://web.archive.org/web/20130127185534/http://archive.newsmax.com/archives/articles/2001/10/30/202458.shtml

140 Jarrah, Mohamed. "Qatar's former emir paid $1 million 'to hide controversial recordings.' Al Arabiya. https://english.alarabiya.net/en/features/2017/06/11/What-were-the-tapes-that-Qatar-s-former-emir-paid-1-million-for-

141 "Qatar: US Ally or Global Menace? Conference Transcript." Security Studies Group. https://securitystudies.org/qatar-us-ally-or-global-menace-conference-transcript/

[142] Smoltczyk, Alexander. "The Voice of Egypt's Muslim Brotherhood." Der Spiegel. https://www.spiegel.de/international/world/islam-s-spiritual-dear-abby-the-voice-of-egypt-s-muslim-brotherhood-a-745526.html

[143] "Sheikh Yousuf Al-Qaradhawi: Allah Imposed Hitler On the Jews to Punish Them – 'Allah Willing, the Next Time Will Be at the Hand of the Believers'" MEMRI. https://www.memri.org/reports/sheikh-yousuf-al-qaradhawi-allah-imposed-hitler-jews-punish-them---allah-willing-next-time

[144] Tweet from Nervana Mahmoud. https://twitter.com/Nervana_1/status/1130052082894069760

[145] Tweet from MEMRI. https://twitter.com/MEMRIReports/status/1130038755589541889

[146] Tweet from Joel Fischer. https://twitter.com/JFNYC1/status/1130259633262792704

[147] Tweet from Asra Nomani. https://twitter.com/AsraNomani/status/1130312327205666816

[148] Folkenflick, David. "Clinton Lauds Virtues Of Al Jazeera: 'It's Real News'" NPR. https://www.npr.org/sections/thetwo-way/2011/03/03/134243115/clinton-lauds-virtues-of-al-jazeera-its-real-news

[149] Baird, Benjamin and Clifford Smith. "How Al Jazeera is avoiding registering as a foreign entity." Washington Examiner. https://www.washingtonexaminer.com/opinion/op-eds/how-al-jazeera-is-avoiding-registering-as-a-foreign-entity

[150] Thrall, Nathan. "How the Battle Over Israel and Anti-Semitism Is Fracturing American Politics." New York Times. https://www.nytimes.com/2019/03/28/magazine/battle-over-bds-israel-palestinians-antisemitism.html

[151] "Governments & Foundations." International Crisis Group. https://www.crisisgroup.org/support-us/our-supporters/governments-foundations

152 Dettmer, Jamie. "Qatar's Foundation for Hypocrisy." Daily Beast. https://www.thedailybeast.com/qatars-foundation-for-hypocrisy

153 "Company Credit Report: Qatar Foundation For Education, Science And Community Development." Cedar Rose. https://securitystudies.org/wp-content/uploads/2019/02/Qatar-Foundation-Credit-Report.pdf

154 Lipton, Eric and Brooke Williams and Nicholas Confessore. "Foreign Powers Buy Influence at Think Tanks." https://www.nytimes.com/2014/09/07/us/politics/foreign-powers-buy-influence-at-think-tanks.html?_r=0

155 Smith, Lee. "How Peace Negotiator Martin Indyk Cashed a Big, Fat $14.8 Million Check From Qatar." https://www.tabletmag.com/sections/israel-middle-east/articles/martin-indyk-qatar

156 "Brookings Responds to Tablet Piece on Qatar Funding." Tablet. https://www.tabletmag.com/sections/news/articles/brookings-responds-to-tablet-piece-on-qatar-funding

157 Schachtel, Jordan. "Many of CNN's national security analysts have undisclosed ties to oppressive Qatari regime." Conservative Review. https://www.conservativereview.com/news/many-cnns-national-security-analysts-undisclosed-ties-oppressive-qatari-regime/

158 Rosiak, Luke. "Elite Universities Hide Information On Funding From Ultraconservative Nation Of Qatar." Daily Caller. https://dailycaller.com/2018/12/16/qatar-georgetown-texas-university/

159 Campbell, Andy. "The Media Industry Laid Off A Thousand People In January. It May Not Be Over." Huffinton Post. https://www.huffpost.com/entry/1000-media-layoffs-buzzfeed-huffpost-yahoo-gannett_n_5c4b61a6e4b0e1872d4384b6

160 McCauley, Kevin. "Ogilvy NY Handles US Push for Qatar Foundation." O'Dwyer's PR. https://www.odwyerpr.com/story/public/11249/2018-09-05/ogilvy-ny-handles-us-push-for-qatar-foundation.html

[161] Schreckinger, Ben. "Qatar hired ex-Trump campaign staffer as D.C. lobbyist." Politico. https://www.politico.com/story/2019/02/23/qatar-stuart-jolly-trump-campaign-1182279

[162] The Doha Forum on Facebook. https://www.facebook.com/watch/?v=376571413107433

[163] Schachtel, Jordan. "NeverTrump's new base of operations: Qatar?" Conservative Review. https://www.conservativereview.com/news/nevertrumps-new-base-of-operations-qatar/

[164] Reaboi, David. "Qatar Hacking Scandal Illustrates How U.S. Media Megaphones Foreign Agitprop." The Federalist. https://thefederalist.com/2019/01/31/qatar-hacking-scandal-illustrates-u-s-media-megaphones-foreign-agitprop/

[165] Chizhik-Goldschmidt, Avital. "Is This The Fall Of The Prime Grill Empire?" The Forward. https://forward.com/food/387521/is-this-the-fall-of-the-prime-grill-empire/

[166] Oster, Marcy. "San Diego Hilton Cancels $1M Passover Trip For 700." The Forward. https://forward.com/fast-forward/368365/san-diego-hilton-cancels-1m-passover-trip-for-700/

[167] Rosen, Armin. "Qatar's Efforts to Influence American Jews Continue to Unravel." Tablet. https://www.tabletmag.com/sections/news/articles/qatars-efforts-to-influence-american-jews-continue-to-unravel

[168] Tweet from Jamie Weinstein. https://twitter.com/jamie_weinstein/status/1013859286664073218

[169] Rosen, Armin. "Morton Klein and the Future of American Zionism." Tablet. https://www.tabletmag.com/sections/news/articles/morton-klein-and-the-future-of-american-zionism

170 Pink, Aiden. "Morton Klein Admits Speaking With Alleged Secret Qatari Agent." The Forward. https://forward.com/news/national/406647/morton-klein-admits-speaking-with-alleged-secret-qatari-agent/

171 "ZOA: U.S. State Department Should Designate Qatar A State-Sponsor of Terrorism, and Suspend Qatar Airways FAA License – Unless Qatar Ceases Its Financial Support of Hamas." Zionist Organization of America. https://zoa.org/2014/08/10256037-256037/

172 Dershowitz, Alan. "Why is Qatar being blockaded and isolated?" The Hill. https://thehill.com/opinion/international/368764-why-is-qatar-being-blockaded-and-isolated

173 Byrkowicz, Julie. "The New Lobbying: Qatar Targeted 250 Trump 'Influencers' to Change U.S. Policy." Wall Street Journal. https://www.wsj.com/articles/the-new-lobbying-qatar-targeted-250-trump-influencers-to-change-u-s-policy-1535554647?mod=e2tw

174 "US-Qatar Business Council & US Chamber Host Reception to Honor Amir of Qatar." US-Qatar Business Council. https://www.usqbc.org/news/us-qatar-business-council-us-chamber-host-reception-to-honor-amir-of-qatar

175 "Lobbyist sued by Trump fundraiser ends work for Qatar." Associated Press. https://www.reuters.com/article/us-usa-trump-russia-qatar/lobbyist-sued-by-trump-fundraiser-ends-work-for-qatar-idUSKCN1J328A

176 Frantzman, Seth. "How Qatar's Jewish strategy backfired." Jerusalem Post. https://www.jpost.com/Middle-East/How-Qatars-Jewish-strategy-backfired-560586

177 Ettinger, Yair. "Why is the Head of the OU Kashrut Department in Qatar?" Jerusalem Post. https://www.jpost.com/diaspora/why-is-the-head-of-the-ou-kashrut-department-in-qatar-513532

178 Reaboi, David. "Khashoggi: Qatari Asset in Life; Qatari Asset in Death." Security Studies Group. https://securitystudies.org/jamal-khashoggi-and-qatar-in-the-echo-chamber (2018)

[179] "Why Is The US Media Destroying the US-Saudi Relationship?" Security Studies Group. https://securitystudies.org/reaboi-in-al-riyadh-why-is-the-us-media-destroying-the-us-saudi-relationship (2018)

[180] Smith, Lee. "For Obama, Iran Talks Are Also About Testing the Limits of American Jewish Power." https://www.tabletmag.com/sections/israel-middle-east/articles/obama-and-american-jewish-power Tablet. (2013)

[181] Barnes, Julian E., Eric Schmitt and David D. Kirkpatrick. "'Tell Your Boss': Recording Is Seen to Link Saudi Crown Prince More Strongly to Khashoggi Killing." New York Times. https://www.nytimes.com/2018/11/12/world/middleeast/jamal-khashoggi-killing-saudi-arabia.html

[182] "Washington Post reveals how Qatar Foundation shaped their pieces by Khashoggi." Al-Jazeera. https://english.alarabiya.net/en/features/2018/12/23/Washington-Post-reveals-how-Qatar-Foundation-shaped-their-pieces-by-Khashoggi.html

[183] Mekhennet, Souad and Greg Miller. "Jamal Khashoggi's final months as an exile in the long shadow of Saudi Arabia." Washington Post. https://www.washingtonpost.com/world/national-security/jamal-khashoggis-final-months-an-exile-in-the-long-shadow-of-saudi-arabia/2018/12/21/d6fc68c2-0476-11e9-b6a9-0aa5c2fcc9e4_story.html?noredirect=on

[184] "Time Person of the Year 2018: The Guardians and the War on Truth." Time Magazine. https://time.com/person-of-the-year-2018-the-guardians/

[185] Mekhennet, Souad and Greg Miller. "Jamal Khashoggi's final months as an exile in the long shadow of Saudi Arabia." Washington Post. https://www.washingtonpost.com/world/national-security/jamal-khashoggis-final-months-an-exile-in-the-long-shadow-of-saudi-arabia/2018/12/21/d6fc68c2-0476-11e9-b6a9-0aa5c2fcc9e4_story.html?noredirect=on

[186] Hanson, Jim. "The US-Saudi relationship must be preserved – our national interest demands it." Fox News. https://www.foxnews.com/opinion/the-us-saudi-relationship-must-be-preserved-our-national-interest-demands-it

[187] "Hanson: Beware of Media Spin about Khashoggi; We Need to Make Decisions on KSA Soberly." Security Studies Group. https://securitystudies.org/hanson-beware-of-media-spin-about-khashoggi-we-need-to-make-decisions-on-ksa-soberly/

[188] Brodsky, Matthew RJ. "Why is the media ignoring the most glaring questions about Jamal Khashoggi?" Spectator US. https://spectator.us/media-jamal-khashoggi (2018)

[189] Costa, Robert and Karoun Demirjan. "Conservatives mount a whisper campaign smearing Khashoggi in defense of Trump." Washington Post. https://www.msn.com/en-au/news/world/conservatives-mount-a-whisper-campaign-smearing-khashoggi-in-defense-of-trump/ar-BBOANfD?li=AAgfIYZ&%253Bocid=mailsignoutmd

[190] Wittes, Tamara Cofman. "On Jamal Khashoggi, the Muslim Brotherhood, and Saudi Arabia." Brookings Institution. https://www.brookings.edu/blog/order-from-chaos/2018/10/19/on-jamal-khashoggi-the-muslim-brotherhood-and-saudi-arabia/

[191] Patty, Brad and Nick Short. "Firehoses in the Jamal Khashoggi Case: An Analysis of an Information Operation." Security Studies Group. http://securitystudies.org/wp-content/uploads/2018/11/SSG-Firehoses-in-the-Khashoggi-Case.pdf

[192] "How the man behind Khashoggi murder ran the killing via Skype." Reuters. https://www.reuters.com/article/us-saudi-khashoggi-adviser-insight/how-the-man-behind-khashoggi-murder-ran-the-killing-via-skype-idUSKCN1MW2HA

[193] Tweet from David Reaboi. https://twitter.com/davereaboi/status/1069248357707759616 (December 2, 2018)

ABOUT THE AUTHOR

David Reaboi works at the intersection of communications and policy, specializing in national security, political warfare, influence operations, and the media.

When conservative activist and publisher Andrew Breitbart wanted to create a national security-focused website in 2010, he turned to David to launch and helm Big Peace. Since that time, he has created and grown more than 20 websites and online publishing platforms, as well as run dozens of public policy and communications campaigns.

In addition, he is the president of **STRATEGIC IMPROVISATION**, a communications company focused on developing and executing impactful and flexible strategies for a variety of clients in the national security world.

David received a BA from George Washington University in International Affairs, with a concentration in the history of the Cold War. He is a Claremont Institute Lincoln Fellow, a Senior Fellow at the Center for Security Policy, and has ghostwritten or contributed to several book about Sunni Islamist movements.

His work appears regularly at American Greatness, The Federalist, Claremont Review of Books, The Washington Times, Jewish Journal, Human Events, The American Mind, RedState, PJMedia, and elsewhere.

He lives in Miami Beach.

Made in the USA
Columbia, SC
30 March 2021